CHURCH THAT WORKS

YOUR ONE-STOP RESOURCE FOR EFFECTIVE MINISTRY

GARY L. MCINTOSH

BakerBooks
Grand Rapids, Michigan

Other books by Gary L. McIntosh

Biblical Church Growth
The Exodus Principle
Look Back, Leap Forward
Make Room for the Boom . . . or Bust
One Church, Four Generations
One Size Doesn't Fit All
Staff Your Church for Growth

With Robert Edmondson
It Only Hurts on Monday

With Sam Rima
Overcoming the Dark Side
   of Leadership

With Glen Martin
Creating Community
Finding Them, Keeping Them
The Issachar Factor

© 2004 by Gary L. McIntosh

Published by Baker Books
a division of Baker Publishing Group
P.O. Box 6287, Grand Rapids, MI 49516-6287
www.bakerbooks.com

Printed in the United States of America

Library of Congress Cataloging-in-Publication Data
McIntosh, Gary, 1947–
    Church that works : your one-stop resource for effective ministry / Gary L. McIntosh.
       p.   cm.
    ISBN 0-8010-9161-6 (pbk.)
    1. Church management. I. Title.
BV652.M425 2004
245—dc22   2004005399

Scripture is taken from the New American Standard Bible®, Copyright © 1960, 1962, 1963, 1968, 1971, 1972, 1973, 1975, 1977, 1995 by The Lockman Foundation. Used by permission.

Contents

INTRODUCTION

Cold linoleum floors, sterile stainless steel pans, and strange medicinal smells—I never liked going to the doctor's office. When I was a child, the doctor's office always seemed to go hand in hand with shots. And I did not like shots!

In fourth grade my view of doctors and shots changed. I became sick at school and, after going home, was even too sick to go to the doctor's office. Fortunately for me, in those days doctors still made house calls, bringing along their little black bag of medicines. So my mother called the doctor, and he came to our house very late at night.

As it turned out, I had a severe case of strep throat, for which the doctor needed to give me a penicillin shot. I was so sick I never even felt the shot. It was three weeks before I returned to school. Looking back on that experience, I am thankful for that doctor and his little black bag.

Today's church leaders find that they often need diagnoses and prescriptions that will assist in building a healthy church. Of course not every church needs emergency care like I did. Yet every church can benefit from preventative care. That's why I've written *Church That Works: Your One-Stop Resource for Effective Ministry.* It is a unique collection of the best in descriptive and prescriptive care for a local church. Consider it your own little black bag, containing numerous ideas, insights, and concepts to help your church stay healthy.

In *Church That Works* you have the benefit of your own personal consultant (church doctor) right in your own hands. You can profit from the expertise and insight that have helped numerous churches in the United States and Canada stay or become healthy. These are innovative approaches that many top church consultants use and that you can adopt immediately for use in your own church. Here are a few of the topics in this book:

- the danger signs of decline
- how to turn a church around
- what guests see when they come to your church
- steps for initiating multiple services
- insights for relocating a church
- ideas for negotiating your salary

And there are many more practical insights and creative ideas for today's complex ministry.

Church That Works is a compilation of articles that were originally published in the *Church Growth Network* newsletter. They have been edited to fit together in this unique resource. Since 1989 the *Church Growth Network* has reported and analyzed the latest research in church ministry. These short, insightful, and action-oriented articles cut through the avalanche of information available to deliver the best solutions for faithful ministry.

You'll want to keep *Church That Works* near at hand for practical advice at a glance as you tackle the challenges facing today's church. Each chapter takes only minutes to read but provides a wealth of thought-provoking ideas for ministry. Look over the table of contents and read whatever article attracts your interest. Or take time to read one article a week, meditating on the depth of implications found in each one.

Whether you are a pastor, church leader, or other person who cares deeply for your church, as you read this book, you will be accessing proven insights—without having to do extensive research. This book will prove to be an invaluable guide for decision making.

PART 1

BUILDING
FOUNDATIONS

1

The Speed of Change

A recent joke tells of a college freshman stopping a young lady who was hurrying to class. "What's the rush?" he asks. "I've got to get to class before the textbook goes out of date," she replies.

Our Fast-Changing Society

While the joke overstates our current situation, we must admit change is taking place at a faster pace than in years past. Here are a few examples of how change is occurring with greater and greater frequency:

- In 1979 Sony Corporation invented the Walkman. To date the company has developed more than 227 different models.
- New models of computers are often out of date within 120 days and discontinued within one year.

- In 1971 the average American was targeted by at least 560 daily advertising messages. Today we receive 3,000-plus messages per day.
- In the early 1990s it took 7.5 days to manufacture a computer. Now it requires only a few hours.
- Since 1987 the number of fax machines in U.S. offices has increased by 10,000,000.
- Since 1983 the number of computers in U.S. offices has increased by 25,000,000.

Our Appropriate Response

One of the most consistent aspects of life is change. Thus to grow and develop in this fast-paced society, we must move with it. Here are a few ideas on how we can face the speed of change:

Realize change is part of God's design. The world has been in motion ever since God created it. While God personally does not change, the creation changes regularly. Remember, God appointed mankind to manage the earth's resources, which includes managing change in an appropriate manner rather than resisting it.

Learn on the fly, forever. Once upon a time a basic education prepared a person for a lifetime of work and ministry. Today basic education is effective for ten to fifteen years at most. Continuing education is today's watchword. Learn as you go from every source that you know.

Rescript challenges. In Chinese the word for *crisis* is derived from two different symbols. One represents despair, the other opportunity. Rescripting means looking for the opportunities rather than the difficulties in the changes around us.

Focus on your core. People can live with change all around them if there is a changeless core within them. Spend time developing the spiritual center of your life. Take time each day to read God's Word, meditate, and pray. In addition, take a few moments to walk or listen to birds or watch clouds or listen to your favorite music or read a book of poetry.

Rightsize your life. Reorganize your life by getting rid of unnecessary work or involvements. Only about 20 percent of what we do is really necessary. We choose to do the rest. Take time to consider how you can scale back. You can probably eliminate some board and committee meetings, extra assignments from work, or habits, like watching television.

Empower those around you. Give those around you more power to make decisions on their own without your input or permission. Speed up meetings by asking those under your supervision to bring problems *and* solutions when they meet with you. Resist the temptation to be an active participant in all meetings and activities.

Live by your mission statement. To be effective, a mission statement should be twenty-five words or less in length. Write one and then evaluate all that you do against your statement. If an activity does not fit into your mission statement, consider not doing it.

The speed of change is not likely to slow down in the years ahead. To be effective in our lives and in the Lord's work, we must learn to manage our time well.

2

A New Social Contract

Questions of church ministry are ultimately social questions. They involve how people work together and interact. While the exact details are still being worked out, the changes in the social contract under which churches, senior pastors, and staff members minister is taking on a different form and dimension early in the twenty-first century.

Aspects of the New Social Contract

It is clear that churches are expecting much more from their staff members than in previous decades. Today churches look to hire staff members with a portfolio of skills and competencies that is larger than was required just a decade ago. Counterbalancing the church's changing expectations, staff members look for increased appreciation and an enriching environment in which to minister. When the new social contract will be settled is anyone's guess. However, five broad ideas will likely be major aspects of it.

A Clear Direction

Purpose, vision, and *values* are three buzz words we often heard in churches during the past decade. However, they are words that speak to real substance, because only the churches that have a clear sense of direction will see much growth in the coming decades. It makes sense that effective staff teams must be committed to their church's purpose, vision, and values.

To gain such a commitment, however, the new social contract suggests that staff members must take an active part in creating the purpose, vision, and values of the churches they serve. This involves not only the development of the purpose, vision, and values but also an understanding of how these elements align with their personal purpose, vision, and values.

A Learning Environment

Under the new social contract, staff members are selected not for what they already know but for how fast they can learn. It is not so important to be able to access information in the twenty-first century but to be able to differentiate between relevant information and the exponentially multiplying masses of nonrelevant information. This means that constant training will be the norm. Churches that hope to fulfill Christ's mission to reach the lost must provide for ongoing staff training with a variety of programs, such as sabbaticals, continuing education, and seminars.

Additionally, under the new social contract, churches must be willing to let staff members innovate and attempt creative new ministries. Just as the last half of the twentieth century was a time of organization, the first half of the twenty-first century is a time of innovation. Churches and staff members will excel by demonstrating a high degree of flexibility and adaptability in dealing with people, technology, and the changing ministry environment.

Most important will be an ability to remain connected to people. Today's staff members look for a church that gives them greater freedom to learn and try new ministries. They desire an environment where they can take disciplined risks to develop new ministry forms and styles.

A Challenging Atmosphere

From all appearances, social and spiritual forces will continue to create ongoing change that will demand more from churches and staff members. Some researchers have predicted that the changes we experience in our current decade will be more extreme than the changes experienced between 1900 and 2000. If this is true, church leaders will be faced with rethinking staff competencies and a fundamental redefinition of working relationships.

The new social contract requires churches to hold staff members accountable to higher levels of excellence and performance, but in doing so churches must provide the necessary resources for success. In addition to the obvious resources of office, up-to-date equipment, and an above-average budget are a stimulating ministry environment, an understanding of the needs of staff members, and a church of which staff members can be proud to dedicate themselves.

A Connected Relationship

The new social contract calls for churches to realize that most professionals in all fields have computers on their desks and cell phones in their pockets. Technology allows staff to connect with others almost anywhere and anytime.

While most people live, work, and play in the midst of millions of others, there still is a basic disconnect that leaves many people feeling lonely. For church staffs to operate successfully, they must be resourced with up-to-date technology to remain connected to people, who may be removed from them in space, thought, or emotion.

A Sense of Appreciation

In a rapidly changing world an excellent staff will be a prime ingredient of church growth, so churches must accommodate staff members' desire for self-fulfillment.

Under the new social contract, staff members must receive appropriate appreciation and recognition. Three core issues that staff members look for are fair compensation, relevant feedback, and recognition for their contribution. To balance these desires, staff members must willingly accept accountability to a high level of performance, effort, and excellence.

Ministry Teams

The challenge of growing a fruitful church ministry in the next few decades is significant. What may be required above all is a fundamental rethinking of the need for, value of, and approach to team ministry. The changing face of ministry demands interdependent teams, because few individuals will be capable of knowing or doing it all.

The main challenge for churches is finding and keeping excellent staff members. This will require a balancing of different interests—a new social contract.

As you think about your church and consider some of the changes that have recently taken place, what do you think is likely to change in the next five to ten years? The time is now to begin adjusting to these changes.

3

PRAYER

We are living during one of the greatest prayer revivals of modern history and are seeing prayer done in a variety of ways.

Contemporary Forms of Prayer

The following are twelve prayer trends that may help you think of creative ways to increase prayer in your ministry.

1. *Praying the Scripture.* As we read the Bible, we often sense that God is putting his finger on specific areas of our lives where he wishes to change us, encourage us, or teach us. Using these Scriptures as a pattern for prayer provides a meaningful way for our lives to be reshaped according to his will.
2. *Concerts of prayer.* A concert of prayer is the uniting of the entire local body of Christ in prayer for the things that concern God. It may involve pastors, leaders, and churches—cross-denominationally—in prayer for the spiritual awakening of their community, city, or nation.

3. *Praise.* Emphasizing praise during prayer as a way of worshiping God for who he is and what he does is quite common. Praise helps us focus our heart on God, removes worry and earthly concerns, increases faith, invades Satan's territory, and mobilizes God's power.

4. *On-site praying.* A unique form of on-site prayer is that of flagpole praying. This practice is most common with youth pastors and youth workers who meet quarterly at local high schools for an early-morning time of prayer around the school's flagpole. Praying in the home of a person who is ill is another form of on-site prayer. We can pray for people at church but praying on-site, at the ill person's home, is powerful.

5. *Spiritual warfare.* While there is a wide spectrum of views concerning spiritual warfare, many Christians are becoming more aware of Satan's power and the necessity for training in intercessory prayer. In one sense, all believers invade Satan's territory when they pray. However, a few people are uniquely called to intercede against principalities and powers that afflict people, churches, and, some believe, even nations.

6. *Prayer partners.* Churches are organizing key leadership, including staff, to pray for each other on a rotating basis each quarter. This partnering of people encourages bonding and appreciation of one another.

7. *Small-group prayer.* Some churches divide into prayer groups that meet weekly or once each month in homes. Many use the first Sunday evening of each month for this special purpose.

8. *Prayer seminars.* Prayer seminars are being used today to raise consciousness concerning prayer and to teach people prayer skills. A variety of prayer models and ways to pray are introduced. Usually prayer seminars include a lot of time for prayer and not simply instruction about prayer.

9. *Prayer retreats.* Prayer retreats are being planned and executed with great impact on churches. When people get

away from the everyday routine, they are freed to focus on the still, small voice of God.

10. *Early-morning prayer.* In the first half of the twentieth century, churches began to have prayer meetings on a midweek evening. Now, with many people arriving home from work later than they used to, midweek prayer meeting attendance has been declining. Today churches are finding that early morning is often a better time to meet for prayer.

11. *Identification of intercessors.* Attempts are being made to identify individuals gifted in the area of intercession. These people usually manifest several qualities. They desire to pray at least an hour per day. Accompanying this motivation is an insatiable yearning to read and know more about prayer and to be around people with a like focus. Inevitably, whatever their vision, they will almost always be involved in spiritual warfare.

12. *Team prayer.* The best way to model prayer is through the pastoral staff and leadership teams. As church members see their leaders teaming together in prayer, they are encouraged to follow the same pattern. In many churches staff are encouraged to set aside time each day for prayer as a regular part of their quiet time. Once each week the staff prays together for their church, requests from the congregation, as well as for themselves. Each staff member and leader recruits his or her own prayer team, which covers the leader and his or her ministry in prayer each day.

Practicing Prayer

Just as Jesus modeled prayer to his disciples, we must lead the way in modeling prayer in our church ministries. Try to implement some of the preceding forms of prayer. The following ideas may be helpful.

Pray continually. Prayer must support all we do. It should be a natural thing for us to pray about everything—decisions, problems, and the needs of others. Also we must remember to give thanks and to ask God's blessing and guidance on each ministry activity.

Implementation:

- Renew your commitment to a life of prayer.
- Set a new goal for the length of your prayer time.
- Take time to pray with all people who enter your office.
- Be sensitive to statements of need from your staff, family, friends, and church members.
- Don't just say "I'll pray for you." Take the time right then to offer a word of prayer.

Encourage significant staff and leadership prayer. When church leaders and staff pray, it lets the congregation know they are cared for and provides a model for them to follow.

Implementation:

- Require staff to set aside time each day for personal prayer.
- Once each week, bring the staff together to pray for each other, your church, and the needs of the congregation.

Organize prayer partners. Partnering together for prayer provides a prayer covering for key leaders, strengthening their relationships and appreciation of each other as well as creating a unified working environment.

Implementation:

- Organize key leaders, including staff, into prayer teams to pray for each other on a rotating basis each quarter. For example, you could have two lay leaders and a staff member in a group or three leaders in a group.

- Pray for each leader's personal walk with the Lord, ministry schedule, relationships, moral strength, and finances.

Integrate prayer into your small groups. Small groups are an excellent place for leaders to model prayer, develop closer bonds, and encourage church members.

Implementation:

- Give each person the opportunity to share prayer requests and answers to prayer in his or her life.
- Provide a list of general concerns or requests for the corporate body.
- Allow ten minutes to half an hour of group time for prayer.
- Ask each group to read and discuss a selected book on prayer and then begin using the insights in their small group.

Make prayer an agenda item. Generate a heart for seeking God's wisdom, guidance, and will by spending a significant time in prayer at the beginning of each meeting. Not only will this put prayer into its proper place in the structure of a meeting, but it will also lead the members into a common understanding of God's will and direction.

Implementation:

- Put prayer on the agenda!
- Suggest that prayer be focused on the specific areas to be discussed and covered.
- Take a short prayer break whenever you sense that time in the meeting is being wasted or friction is beginning to develop.

Conduct prayer seminars. While modeling is the best way to train people, prayer seminars are a superb way to teach and involve people in prayer quickly.

Implementation:

- Schedule a seminar at least every other year on the basics of prayer.
- Encourage leaders and staff to attend prayer seminars.
- Set aside one third of the seminar time for actual prayer.

Hold leadership prayer retreats. In our busy society it is often difficult for people to find time to pray. Prayer retreats provide time to relax, meditate, read God's Word, and pray.

Implementation:

- Hold weekend prayer retreats with leadership alone or with leadership and laity prayer partners.
- Teach and model various prayer styles and provide extended times for prayer.
- Hold prayer retreats, especially when the church faces major decisions.

Offer early-morning prayer times. One way to provide a fresh approach for general prayer is early-morning prayer times. This is especially desirable when the traditional prayer meeting is nonexistent or poorly attended. When a variety of meeting times for prayer is offered, new people who are not attending the midweek prayer meeting will become involved.

Implementation:

- When feasible, open your church during early-morning hours for people to come for prayer.
- If there is space, set aside a room specifically designated for prayer.
- Make prayer requests available from church members, missionaries, and church leaders.

- Provide a topical counseling book so those with prayer burdens can look up Scriptural and godly wisdom.

Develop prayer opportunities in Sunday school. Encourage teachers to take time to pray in each Sunday school class. Ask youth and adult classes to schedule a quarterly prayer Sunday for teaching about and practicing prayer, as well as an annual class prayer retreat.

Implementation:

- Offer an adult elective course on prayer.
- Encourage classes to pray for each other's needs.
- Challenge all Sunday school teachers to get to know the needs of each class member and to pray specifically for him or her.

Encourage leaders to make use of prayer resources. Books, tapes, and articles on prayer are excellent resources for broadening leaders' vision, knowledge, and understanding of the intricacies of prayer. Leaders will gain a greater appreciation for the importance of prayer in their particular area of leadership.

Implementation:

- Start a prayer library.
- Suggest books for leaders to buy and read. Then hold discussions at staff and leadership meetings on the content, stressing application to their own life and ministry.
- Encourage leaders to share what they learn with the people to whom they minister.

The times are changing, but increasingly prayer will be the power supply and the fuel for effective ministry. Those who use it wisely and often will find they are able to reach their God-given goals and will be victorious in the spiritual battles they encounter.

PART 2

CHANGING TIMES

4

Sixty-Five Years of Television

The first flickering television images hit the airwaves on April 30, 1939. President Franklin D. Roosevelt gave a short speech to open the New York World's Fair. It was the first public broadcast of an electronic medium called television.

Roosevelt's speech was aired by the Radio Corporation of America (RCA). At that time, fewer than one hundred sets of the new "picture radio" had been sold. The screens ranged in size from five to twelve inches.

The Early Years

The first daily television broadcast was from Radio City in Manhattan. The first portable black-and-white TV was introduced in 1956. The first battery-powered set appeared in 1960. In 1966 NBC became the first network to televise all programs in color.

Here are a few other interesting firsts:

- First televised sporting event—a college baseball game between Columbia and Princeton on May 17, 1939

- First televised Major League Baseball game—the Cincinnati Reds and Brooklyn Dodgers on August 26, 1939
- First televised newscast—December 7, 1941, as the Columbia Broadcasting System (CBS) reported the events of Pearl Harbor

The Future

Today we have high-definition television (HDTV), which offers a sharp picture, rich color, and compact-disc (CD) sound quality.

Fiber-optic cables may be attached to phone lines resulting in a universal system whereby subscribers can do business and choose a myriad of programs. Potentially it could make network and cable TV obsolete.

Almost science fiction, the prediction of some is that we will soon see imaging—a system whereby viewers can see themselves in clothes without actually trying them on—and holograms—a system whereby small, three-dimensional figures act out a scene on the living room floor.

TV's Impact on Ministry

In the sixty-five years since its formal debut, television has become a primary entertainment medium, chronicler of history, wellspring of popular culture, major force for political and social change, coercive commercial vehicle, and powerful disseminator of information.

Because of television's pervasive influence, it will continue to have a strong impact on our culture. Here are some ways that television has affected us, followed by some ideas about how we should respond:

Immediate satisfaction. Products are sold, complex issues are solved, and victory is won in thirty minutes on TV.

In our television-saturated culture, people tend to expect that life will give the same immediate results. The ideas of delayed gratification and a process of spiritual growth are not well accepted.

Our response:

- Preach character sketches of biblical people. Point out the process each took to mature in their faith.
- Share examples of people who waited for prayers to be answered, personal problems to be solved, and personal growth to occur.

Increasing boredom. TV gives the impression that life moves at a fast pace. This impression tends to produce boredom and lack of determination when it comes to staying with tasks and learning mundane lessons in everyday life. Subconsciously people compare the real world with the fast-paced, action-oriented pulse beat of a TV series.

Our response:

- Streamline your worship services so that they move along without down time.
- Schedule classes, small groups, and Bible studies in shorter time blocks.
- Preach shorter sermon series. You may find that a six-week series works better than a thirteen-week series.

Consumer mentality. Spending on TV advertising soared from $171 million in 1950 to more than $1.6 billion in 1960. It increased to $3.6 billion in 1970, $11.4 billion in 1980, $32 billion in 1989, and $40 billion in 1999. Television has taught Americans to buy all they see and charge what they can't afford.

Our response:

- Stress biblical stewardship of time, talent, and treasure.
- Encourage worshipers to use their money in ways that have eternal value.
- Provide practical workshops on managing money.
- Preach a minimum of six stewardship messages a year.

Common knowledge. I Love Lucy, Gunsmoke, American Bandstand, The Mickey Mouse Club, The Cosby Show, Life Goes On, and numerous other TV shows have provided the viewing public with a common base of symbols, fads, and experiences unknown in times past.

Our response:

- Use examples from TV shows rather than illustration books to illustrate sermons. Most congregations will understand illustrations from their favorite TV series, gaining a good understanding of the point you are making.

Short attention span. TV commercials and programs have created in us a short attention span. Car chases and other rapidly changing scenes have taught viewers to concentrate for only about thirty seconds.

Our response:

- Move away from the pulpit, rather than standing in one place during the sermon.
- Preach without notes so that your message seems more spontaneous.
- Vary your volume and pitch.
- Use visuals.

- Organize your message into seven-minute blocks, changing to a new point in each block.

Personal touch. The relational aspects of communication are up and transfer of content is down. Simply making contact is more important to people than conveying information. Letter writing is diminishing, with the phone call taking its place. The motto "Reach out and touch someone" expresses this fundamental change, and the popularity of e-mail messages, instant messaging, text messaging, and faxing one another all highlight the importance of personal touch through communication.

Our response:

- Deliver your sermon from the floor, close to the people, rather than from the platform, removed from the people.
- Communicate content in one-on-one fashion through stories that touch the lives of people.

Multiple story lines. TV writers often weave two or three story lines into a thirty-minute episode. Sermons usually follow a sequential 1-2-3 format. We no longer live in a sequential world. People carry on many activities at one time.

Our response:

- Weave at least two story lines into your teaching. For example, use a personal story woven together with Jesus' teaching on a certain subject.

In-and-out mentality. TV has taught us that we can step into an episode and it will stand alone. Even the soaps, with their continuing story lines from week to week, have weekly stories that can stand alone.

Our response:

- People hate "to be continued" endings. If you preach a series, keep it short (six weeks).
- Make sure each sermon can stand alone.

Concern for causes. A new word—dramady—has been coined to name a combination of comedy and drama that addresses topics like AIDS, drugs, and sex but does it within a comedic setting. TV has started facing tough issues and trying to provide answers. For example, diverse shows like *Seventh Heaven* and *Law and Order* deal with real-life issues that were often ignored by television shows in years gone by.

Our response:

- Tastefully include current issues in your sermons.
- Don't make a habit of dealing with heavy issues each week, but don't be afraid of addressing them either.

5

THE INFORMATION AGE

Social scientists have identified three distinct ages that can serve as a brief outline of history:

The Agricultural Age—the time period that spans most of known history to about 1860, named for the main occupation that involved more than 90 percent of all workers—farming. The main context was the small rural town. The key unit was the extended family.

The Industrial Age—the time period from 1860 to about 1956, named for the growth of industrial factories. The main context was the city. The key unit was the nuclear family.

The Information Age—the time period from 1956 to the present, named for the rapid growth of technology. The main context is the world. The key unit is the fractured family.

A Data Overload

The Information Age in which we now live has created an overload of data that overwhelms most people. Consider a few implications:

Travel. In 1914 the typical American averaged 2,640 miles per year in travel. Today the average car owner averages 10,000 miles per year with some traveling 30,000 or more miles per year! Many people will travel more than 3,000,000 miles in their lifetime.

Implication: People are tired, have less free time, and are more difficult to recruit as ministry volunteers.

Change. The world today is as different from fifty years ago as 1950 was from the time of Julius Caesar. Within a couple of decades the share of the industrialized nations' workforce that is engaged in manufacturing will be no more than 5 to 10 percent. "Knowledge workers" will take their place.

Implication: People oppose change, resist making friends, and wonder why they are lonely.

Saturation. In one year the average American will read or complete 3,000 notices and forms, read 100 newspapers and 36 magazines, watch 2,463 hours of television, listen to 730 hours of radio, buy 20 CDs, talk on the telephone almost 61 hours, and read 3 books.

Implication: People hear so much noise, so much "informational cacophony," that they are not going to hear what you say.

Specialization. The sheer volume of data makes it inevitable that people focus on the narrow endeavor. Our information explosion results in a fragmentation of knowledge leading to specialization, overspecialization, and subspecialization.

Implication: People cannot see the big picture, tie the ends together, or see how the pieces relate.

Memory. People are plagued with "Chinese-dinner" memory dysfunction! They forget what they learn within one hour! An emphasis on short-term memory, characterized by cramming unnecessary information for unnecessary tests to get unnecessary grades, affects every area of life.

Implication: People hear information, learn it, and lose it without its having much effect on their lives.

Inaccuracies. The General Accounting Office of the IRS found that of the letters written to the IRS by people with tax questions, 53 percent were answered correctly, 31 percent of the answers contained major errors, and 16 percent were unclear or incomplete. When the IRS received phone calls, 36 percent of the callers were given wrong answers! Providing inaccurate information is characteristic of many of our public and private institutions.

Implication: People know information is out there, have difficulty getting it, and make mistakes without it.

Amnesia. Overload amnesia results when the brain shuts down to protect itself from too much incoming information. With this malady, people cannot recall even simple information, such as a friend's name when trying to introduce him or her to another person. This often happens in classrooms, conferences, lectures, and while attending church.

Implication: People hear more than they understand, forget what they already know, and resist learning more.

Confusion. Everyone knows what it's like to buy a high-technology product, such as a VCR, get it home, and not understand how to program it. There are other areas of confusion in contemporary life—maneuvering on the Internet or completing IRS forms, for example. Each new form the IRS adds for income tax preparation reportedly adds an additional twenty minutes of time for completion.

Implication: People don't know how to use what they learn, make mistakes when they try, and feel guilty about it.

Insights for Ministry

The models of ministry developed in the Agricultural and Industrial Ages are colliding head-on with the Information Age. Pastors and church leaders are under pressure to develop new models of effective ministry. In general, churches must begin to turn their attention toward making information understandable, rather than simply dumping more data on their people.

The following are a few insights local churches should consider as they seek to minister effectively in the Information Age.

Develop high-touch ministries. "High tech–high touch" is the new phrase of the Information Age. A university study found that students were able to retain information longer in a library when librarians made contact with them, lightly touching their arm while they answered questions. This implies that churches should:

- Place an emphasis on relationships.
- Expand small groups.
- Use counseling centers.
- Train members in the Stephen Ministries (Stephen Ministries is a proven training program to help Christians care for others, inside and outside the church. For information, contact Stephen Ministries, 2045 Innerbelt Business Center Dr., St. Louis, MO 63114-5765, 314-428-2600, www.christcare.com).

Offer a variety of ministries. MOPS (Mothers of Preschoolers), divorce recovery, and never-married singles groups are a few of the new ministries being developed in many churches. New ones are continually needed. To add quality ministries, churches should:

- Employ workers who are specialists in their field.
- Present Bible studies that speak to felt needs.

- Target new groups with new ministries.
- Offer ministries away from church facilities.

Remain flexible. People are busy. In the past a husband would come home from work to a meal his wife had prepared. Today he finds a note on the kitchen counter that reads, "Honey, if you get home before I do, please start dinner." In light of the busy schedules of most members, churches should:

- Conduct services at alternative times on Sunday.
- Expand opportunities for worship and ministry throughout the week.
- Hold a Friday or Saturday evening service.
- Shorten services.

Establish a clear purpose. The demands of keeping a church going often take precedence over pursuing the basic purpose of the church. Ideas, however, do not come from maintenance but from conviction of purpose that burns in the heart and spreads to others. To keep the purpose in the forefront, churches should:

- Clarify their purpose.
- Present ideas in concrete terms rather than philosophical ones.
- Increase ownership of the purpose through regular communication.
- Use real-life stories to illustrate the living out of the purpose.

Keep it simple. Pastors labor under the misconception that it is better to have too much information than to have too little. Years ago psychologist George Miller found that only seven pieces of information, such as digits of a telephone number, can be held easily in a person's short-term memory. In light of the overwhelming amount of information in contemporary society, churches should:

- Simplify communication to the congregation by using e-mail and short notes.
- Make sermons clearer and shorter.
- Make church traffic patterns, instructions concerning upcoming events, and signs obvious.
- Publicly announce only what is of interest to everyone.

Practice good communication. A survey done by the Opinion Research Corporation found that fewer than half of employees rated their companies favorably as to their success in keeping employees informed about what was going on in the company. Executives rate communication problems as their chief difficulty. To avoid these problems, churches should:

- Tie communication to images. Use pictures that illustrate what you are trying to say.
- Use stories, since half of our learning comes in the form of facts and the other in the form of stories and ideas.
- Use humor, since research suggests that putting people in a good mood helps them think through their problems with creativity. Humor relieves stress, allowing people to think clearly.
- Communicate everything in five different ways.

Be patient in decision making. Churches are taking more time to make decisions, being careful and taking the time to search for additional information. A pastoral search used to take three to six months. Today it is taking nine to twelve months. To make decisions, churches should:

- Ask good questions.
- Determine criteria for making a decision before beginning research.
- Use decision-making grids. Form a grid by developing four to six criteria and then match potential options to the criteria.
- Look for consensus rather than unanimous decisions.

Trust others for advice. The book publisher Zondervan produces about 120 books a year but receives as many as 60 manuscripts per week, more than 3,000 submissions a year! And this is just one book company! There is an inability to keep up with the information offered to us through books, newspapers, TV, and the Internet. Leaders must accept the fact that they cannot know it all. Because of this, churches should:

- Use consultants who have expertise in specific areas and a broad base of experience and understanding to interpret information.
- Ask questions, drawing on the knowledge of others.
- Recognize they will never have all the information they would like on a certain issue, so they must stop researching at an appropriate point and make a decision.

Focus on application. People remember only 15 percent of what they hear. George Simmel, a sociologist, was the first to recognize that in urban life people protect themselves from information overload "which results in an incapacity . . . to react to new situations with the appropriate energy." Recognizing the danger of information overload, churches should:

- Focus on known information rather than always giving new information.

- Show people how to do projects rather than simply telling them what to do.
- Concentrate on basic practices instead of on fringe issues.
- Preach and teach on topics that relate to real-life situations.

Emphasize long-term growth. People are being forced to adapt to a new pace of life. In ever shorter time intervals, they must confront novel situations and master new ways of doing things. Churches should:

- Develop home Bible studies that teach people to find information for themselves.
- Give out only the information that people really need to know.
- Use a variety of teaching techniques; not everyone learns the same way.

It's going to get increasingly difficult to interact knowledgeably in our society as the amount of available information expands. Growing churches will be those that make information understandable and practical.

6

1950s versus 2000s

I've got some good news and some bad news for you. The good news is it's a new century and there's great opportunity for ministry. The bad news is some of your people still think it's the 1950s and aren't taking advantage of the ministry opportunities available.

The Opportunity

The Bible encourages: "Conduct yourselves with wisdom toward outsiders, making the most of the opportunity" (Col. 4:5). There is a limited season when people are open to the Good News of Jesus Christ. Our job is to quickly take advantage of the opportunities that are ours to win people to Christ since the season (time) is changing and will not always be available.

The Findings

Music

Music in the 1950s was built on the foundation of hymns, with accompaniment provided primarily by piano and organ.

Music was soft and traditional, unvarying in style, restricted in form and instruments. Choruses were mixed with hymns in the evening service but were a no-no in the morning worship service. A guitar was okay for camp but not church. The choir was always robed, and the song director was mainly a cheerleader who waved his arms in an attempt to excite the people's singing. Amplification was still in its basic stages. Large youth choirs were popular. Music was rarely played during the pastor's prayers.

Music in the 2000s is often built on the foundation of praise songs, accompanied by guitars and a growing variety of other instruments. Music is loud, consisting of praise music mixed with hymns or, in many cases, replacing hymns totally. The new direction is toward worship leaders who help the congregation worship God through singing. Amplification has increasingly improved, but many churches still subsist with old outdated systems. Music is slowly having more of a jazz flavor and acoustic sound. Some churches, however, are going back to quiet hymns.

Facilities

In the 1950s facilities were limited to meeting halls and classrooms, which were designed for a single purpose. Pews were the normal seating provided for worship services. Church architecture gave priority to the place of the sermon with the pulpit up front and elevated, keeping the pastor away from the people. Colors were darker, ceilings were higher, and aisles and pews were longer than they are today. Buildings were smaller, looked churchy, and were sacred. ("Don't run in the Lord's house!" was a common reprimand.)

In the 2000s church facilities are more versatile and include things seldom considered in the 1950s, such as coffee shops and racquetball courts. Movable seating allows for multiple uses of auditoriums. Church architecture stresses relationships by using lighter colors, pews or chairs in a semicircle, and less furniture, effectively bringing the pastor closer to the people. Facilities are more functional; buildings are larger and less churchy—often there are no stained-glass windows or steeple.

Worship Service

In the 1950s the worship service was usually held on Sunday at 11:00 AM—the hour was almost sacred. There was a standard format, something like song, song, Scripture reading, prayer, announcements, song, special music, message, song, altar call, and benediction. Worship was formal with sincerity as the focus. The congregation mainly listened—to the choir, special music, and the sermon. The sermon was topical and viewed as the center of the worship service.

In the 2000s worship is freer flowing with changing formats depending on the theme of the message. Worship now includes drama, interviews, and video. Praise and informality are often emphasized. The sermon is viewed as only a part of worship, with singing and audience participation also considered important. Preaching is often expository, but not necessarily verse by verse. Variable times for worship (multiple services with some offered in the evening during the week) have increased the opportunity of reaching more people. Excellence and authenticity are the focus.

Staffing

In the 1950s there was a large number of volunteers available to carry on the ministry, so the paid staff was minimal, usually just a senior pastor, youth pastor, and music leader. Sometimes there was a children's worker. Senior pastors went into ministry as the result of a clear, divine call and were often jacks-of-all-trades who closely controlled their staffs. Often associates were given responsibility without authority. The number of pastors averaged about one full-time pastor for every three hundred people. Staffing was designed around generalists.

Due in part to the lower number of volunteers, today there are more paid staff members, which may include pastors of singles, women's ministries, drug ministries, senior citizens, as well as leaders of dysfunctional family groups, day school principals, recreational leaders, and preschool directors, to name a few. Staff members are freer to do ministry than in the past but often continue to be given responsibility without authority. Staffs average about one full-time pastor for every 150 to 200 people. Staffing is now based on specialized functions, with some pastors serving out of a vocational choice rather than a sense of call.

Children's Ministry

In the 1950s ministry to children was accomplished primarily through Sunday school, vacation Bible school, and children's choirs. In Sunday school children met in a large group for opening exercises—singing and worship—then divided up into small groups for teaching. Due to the high birth rate of the 1950s, there were more children than there are today, but there was also more volunteer help, since most mothers did not work outside the home and, therefore, could devote time to teaching. A very strict curriculum was used with few visual aids. Children were more literate and disciplined and had lots of contact with adults.

Children's ministry in the 2000s is much more diverse. The children's choir has been replaced by the children's musical, and VBS is losing ground to athletic camps. Other ministries include programs to help working parents, such as year-round child care, preschool ministry, summer and winter camps, as well as day camps. Often children meet in a large group for teaching from a master teacher and then divide up into small groups for interaction. Many children have difficulty reading, are less disciplined, and have less contact with parents and other adults.

Special Programs

In the 1950s one or two weeks were often devoted to missions/ Bible conferences, evangelistic meetings, and youth crusades.

Programs were targeted primarily to church members and were geared to inform. Additional programs tended to be focused around the women's missionary society, the men's work, and youth group. Programming was limited because some issues, such as abortion, homosexuality, and even divorce, were not discussed openly.

Today special programs are often only one or two days long. Special interest groups, such as the underprivileged, unemployed, and other needy categories of people, are the focus of much church programming, while traditional men's and women's programs are less in evidence. Churches are more willing to face difficult social and personal problems and, therefore, more open to developing new ministries for controversial issues, such as dealing with AIDS and divorce recovery. Programs are designed to hold people's attention.

Sunday School

Sunday school in the 1950s was the primary ministry of many churches and was highly departmentalized. A Sunday school superintendent led in opening exercises and then classes were dismissed for study. Sunday school was viewed as an evangelistic arm of the church, since there was less competition for children's time and many children came to Sunday school from unchurched homes. Adults came to Sunday school out of a desire to understand the Bible. Adult classes were typically divided along the lines of gender, age, marital status, topic, or teacher.

Today Sunday school is only one of many ministries, with interest in home groups and weekday or evening small groups on the rise. In today's Sunday schools there is less departmentalization and usually no combined worship time. Often worship is an integral part of the teaching time in each class. Sunday school is viewed as an educational arm of the church, since there is a lot of competition for children's time and children seem to come primarily from Christian homes. People want Sunday school to relate to where they are during the week, learning how the Bible can help them in their personal lives. Adult classes are being divided along the lines of life stage—adults without children, parents with school-age children, parents with adult children, and so on.

International Missions

In the 1950s commitment to foreign missions was the heartbeat of many churches. People not only gave their money but also invested their time in prayer and writing letters to missionaries. Mission policies and goals were not often well thought out, however. Primarily the women in the church determined the church's missionary program, and few pastors would argue with their desires. Missions was primarily an adult concern, and missionaries chose to serve "over there" as a lifelong career. Most went to large nations.

In our churches today there is more awareness of the diversity of needs in missions, but financial and prayer support for missions is often lacking. Mission policies and goals are being examined and well honed by many missions committees. Usually a missions board determines the church's missionary program, and youth play an important part—especially in short-term mission trips. Often the focus of missions is "right here." Abroad, target groups are now smaller, unreached, hidden people groups.

Administration

In the 1950s the pastor was the preacher and general administrator of the church. Because he did it all, church administration was generally weak. Pastors were asked only to be godly, dedicated people, not good managers, and no one had even heard of computers.

Today the pastor often takes the role of leader and visionary, with others being responsible for administration. Therefore administration is more efficient, and the use of computers and other electronic devices is expected. Pastors are asked to be

up to date on the latest ministry tools and to continue formal
education.

Outreach

In the 1950s outreach was easier for a number of reasons.
First, people lived closer to their churches and were more
willing to invite their neighbors. Second, unchurched people
seemed to have a basic understanding of spiritual things,
such as who Jesus Christ is, their own sin, and their need
for redemption. Third, there wasn't the vast diversity of belief
systems common in most communities today. Fourth, people
were sociable and willing to be friends. Evangelism was a high
priority for many churches but their follow-up was often very
weak. Churches had few organized outreach programs and the
ones they had were event-oriented. Most evangelized through
crusades.

In the 2000s outreach is more difficult for a number of reasons. First, people tend to live farther from their church and
find it difficult to invite their neighbors. Second, unchurched
people often don't have even a basic understanding of the
Christian faith. Third, our society has a pluralistic belief system. Fourth, people prefer to be alone and resist socializing.
Though there is more emphasis on follow-up of people, there
is less evangelism taking place. Outreach is being viewed as
more of a lifestyle than simply a church program and is more
relational. Still it remains the ministry of a few faithful.

Welcoming Visitors

In the 1950s people were more sociable and enjoyed being
welcomed at church by formal greeters. Usually the members
of the church were friendly, but little was done to unite newcomers to the church. Most people had to wait months, and
even years, before being able to serve. In the 1950s seven out
of eight adult visitors were people who had grown up in that

church's denomination. Thus they understood the way they did ministry.

In the 2000s people prefer to remain anonymous and may actually resist being greeted. Churches now make more effort to assimilate new people, and people are allowed to serve sooner than in the past. Today only about eight in twenty people who visit a church are familiar with the denomination. Thus there is a greater need for a well-thought-out visitor welcome that helps new people understand a church's ministry.

Ministry

Ministry in the 1950s was tied to formal meetings, and members attended out of a sense of duty or loyalty. Often only a few people in the church did the ministry, which was always well planned and coordinated. Evening services were quite common and the truly dedicated always attended them. There were very few sports programs, and those that existed were for fellowship. Ministry to the elderly had a significant place in a church's overall strategy.

Ministry in the 2000s is more tied to needs, and people are less likely to attend meetings out of duty or loyalty. There is more talk of involving people in ministry, but ministry continues to be done by a few people. Overall, ministries are better planned and there are fewer evening services. Church sports programs are used to reach new people and the unchurched. Unfortunately, much church programming doesn't take seriously the spiritual and physical needs of the elderly.

Prayer

In the 1950s prayer was primarily tied to a midweek meeting. It was viewed as "coming to the throne of grace." There was little or no teaching on how to pray, but prayer was the backbone of the church. Prayer time often included Bible study and the sharing of prayer needs.

Since the late 1980s the interest in prayer has increased and is now often the focus of small groups. Prayer is being viewed as spiritual warfare or a power encounter. However, commitment to prayer is weak in most churches, even though there is more teaching on how to pray.

The work of the church is the work of God, and the organizational system can never compensate for the saving and life-giving work of the Holy Spirit. This single power source for ministry remains, but, as church leaders, we need to distinguish our methods from the surrounding culture and restructure our ministry for effectiveness.

PART 3

CHURCH VISITORS

7

Attracting Guests

While consulting with a small Presbyterian church, I discovered that the church kept an average of 15 percent of its first-time guests. Actually this is just barely below the national average of 16 percent. Further research found that this church attracted only about two guests each month. With an average of twenty-four visitors per year and a 15 percent retention rate, the church added only four new people a year!

This church illustrates a common pattern among churches. It does a fairly good job of keeping people once they come but just doesn't attract enough guests to see much growth. If this church could attract one guest per week, it would add eight new people each year. If it could attract two per week, it would add sixteen people per year.

Preparing for Guests

When you know that guests will be coming to your home for a visit, you spend time cleaning the house, fixing a meal, and generally making the atmosphere as delightful as possible.

In a similar way, before you even begin to ask guests to your church, do some house cleaning.

Develop Your Church's Concern

Is your church good at welcoming new people? If not, it is doubtful that many new people will be attracted to your church.

You can develop your church's concern for new people. Begin by preaching a series of messages on hospitality. Create a profile of the average unchurched man and woman who might attend your church and share it with the congregation. Start a task force to plan better ways to welcome new people. *Hint:* Staff the task force with people who have been in your church less than one year.

Develop Your Church's Morale

The main way guests come to a church is through the invitation of present church attendees. However, if your congregation has low morale, people will not invite others to attend.

You can develop your church's morale. Begin by celebrating positive aspects of your church's ministry. Interview new people from the pulpit. Ask people whose lives have been touched by your church to share their story. Set some reachable goals and praise the congregation when they are reached.

Develop Your Church's Fellowship

Some people attend a church without making many friends. If people in your church do not fellowship with each other, it will be difficult to get them to reach out in fellowship with strangers.

You can develop your church's enjoyment of fellowship. Begin by hosting bimonthly church dinners, encouraging people to share meals with each other on a rotating basis, and scheduling a half-hour fellowship time between the Sunday school and worship service.

Develop Your Church's Welcome

Most churches think they are friendly. However, if newcomers don't feel the same way, you need to improve your welcome.

You can be a friendly church. Begin by being sure that your ushers, parking attendants, and greeters are friendly people. Establish an information center in a place that new people can easily find and staff it with people who will be able to answer their questions.

Set Your Church's Goal

In growing churches, the average percentage of worship attendees who are guests is 4–5 percent. Eventually 20–30 percent of these guests will become members.

You can set a goal for the number of guests you will attract and keep in the next year. Begin by looking over your records for the past one or two years and determine your percentages. If they are as high as those above, rejoice! If not, set a goal to improve your percentages within the next year.

Welcoming Guests

After you've made the necessary preparations, begin to plan ways of attracting new people to your church.

Invitations

Word of mouth is the best way to attract guests to a church. When satisfied people give testimony to others that your church is a great place to attend, you will have all the guests you need.

Here's one way to encourage people to invite others to church. Print a general church business card. Give every person in your church fifty-two cards, and ask each one to give away one card a week with an invitation to attend your church. Remember, one-fourth of nonchurched people say they've never been invited to church.

Rewards

After a church dinner it is customary for the cooks to be thanked for preparing a fine meal. Usually the cooks are invited to come out of the kitchen, and those who have eaten the meal applaud them for their efforts.

Here's one way to reward those who bring new people to church. When you have new people register their attendance, provide a place for them to note who invited them. Keep track of the people who invite others. Host an appreciation dessert once each quarter to honor these key people.

Advertising

If your church is small, just getting off the plateau, or in a location with low visibility, you will need to do something to make your church known to potential guests.

Here's one way to advertise your church: Develop a first-impression piece about your church (see chapter 9 for information on how to do this). At the beginning of the year, mail it to everyone within a five-minute drive of your church. Next year mail it to everyone within a ten-minute drive. Then the third year mail it to everyone within a fifteen-minute drive.

Nonthreatening Entry Points

Because new people often find it uncomfortable to attend a church, growing churches usually offer at least three nonthreatening ways for people to become acquainted with the church.

Here's one way to develop nonthreatening entry points: Ask your regular attendees to list the names of unchurched friends. Then have them list things their friends are interested in, such as sports, classes, crafts, and so on. Group the various interests together, select the three largest groupings, and then during the next year create three new ministries around those three interests.

Welcoming but Not Embarrassing

When guests visit a church, they like to be noticed but want to feel anonymous. If guests are in any way embarrassed, they won't be back.

Here's a good way to welcome guests to church: Begin using the five-minute rule. At the close of your worship service, ask regular attendees to spend five minutes welcoming guests. They should not talk with friends or do any church business during this time. After the benediction or last song, remind the people of the five-minute rule.

It's true! No one ever joins a church without first visiting. So use some of the ideas above and increase your potential for growth by attracting more guests to your church.

8

Starting Good Rumors

Are you looking for a doctor? Do you need a home loan? Are you buying a new car or selecting a college? How do you know which one to choose? Do you look in the paper, watch TV, or "let your fingers do the walking"? If you are like most people, you ask a family member, associate, or friend for his or her advice. Advertisers call this word of mouth. It is the most effective way of advertising any product—even a church!

Biblical Examples

Word-of-mouth advertising is referred to in Scripture as a story, a report, a tiding, a reputation, and a rumor. Rumors are characterized as either good report or evil report (2 Cor. 6:8). Believers are encouraged to think and spread good rumors (Phil. 4:8).

News of Jesus' ministry was mainly communicated by word of mouth. After raising a dead man, Luke records that "this report [rumor, story] concerning Him went out all over Judea and in all the surrounding district" (Luke 7:17).

A classic example of word-of-mouth advertising is found in 1 Thessalonians 1:8. Writing about the church in Thessalonica, Paul says, "For the word of the Lord has sounded forth from you, not only in Macedonia and Achaia, but also in every place your faith toward God has gone forth." People were telling how the Thessalonians had turned from idols to serve a living and true God. They were spreading the story by word of mouth. It was so effective that Paul confesses, "We have no need to say anything."

How Rumors Spread

Studies in the field of diffusion of innovation (how the use of new products spreads) have found that people do not choose a product purely because of factual information. The overwhelming majority of people depend on subjective evaluations from other individuals like themselves who have previously adopted a product. When subjective, positive evaluations are spread through interpersonal networks, the sales of new products literally take off.

In the same way, churches grow as members and attendees model their happiness by spreading good rumors (positive evaluations) to their peers (friends, family, and associates) who are potential adopters. When current members and attendees are satisfied with the ministry of the church, good rumors will develop and spread.

How can a church tie into the network of its members and attendees to reach potential adopters? As a church leader, you do not need to sit by passively. You can be thoughtful, organized, and systematic about word-of-mouth advertising.

The following are some ways your church can begin to develop good rumors for word-of-mouth advertising.

Upgrade facilities. If facilities, grounds, and equipment are below what people would have in their homes, they may not feel good enough about their church to spread good rumors and bring new people. Facilities must be slightly better than people expect.

Enhance services. Services also need to be a notch above expectations and consistently good. For example, if the worship service is excellent about one Sunday per month and mediocre the remaining Sundays, it will be difficult for good rumors to develop. Members will spread good rumors only when they believe that the worship service will be consistently good each Sunday.

Utilize newsletters. A newsletter is a solid way to build a cadre of loyal followers. It is time consuming and expensive but is certainly worth the effort. One key to a successful newsletter is regularity. Many churches put out a newsletter sporadically. If anything, this works against the development of good rumors. The newsletter presentation should be crisp, clean, clear, and upbeat, with good use of photos.

Host open houses. Make it a practice to host regular open house meetings when members can share their desires, hopes, and concerns. At the same meetings church leaders may communicate the church's vision and direction.

Interview people. Interview people from the platform on Sunday mornings. Select new people, those with a fresh testimony, and those who will speak openly about how your church has effectively served them. Host an end-of-the-year event when many people who have been touched by your church may share their stories.

Court opinion leaders. One pastor visited the mayor of his city. After the proper introductions were made, the mayor asked how he could help the pastor. The pastor said he simply wanted to know how the mayor was doing. Before leaving he prayed for the mayor. The mayor was shocked and pleased. Needless to say, this opinion leader has good things to say about this pastor and his church.

Build good experiences. Complete projects that are started. Work on small goals that are sure to succeed and publicize them when they are met. Take slides and pictures of church events, and show them at meetings throughout the year. Develop a video about your church.

Communicate victories. Print answers to prayer in the church program or newsletter. Share how your church is progressing toward its yearly goals and tell about ministries that are reaching people. Publicly read thank-you cards and letters from people who have been helped by your church. Remember to communicate victories in five different ways so that people will remember them.

Develop a sense of expectancy. Preach messages that point to hope in the Lord. Describe how God has met church needs over the years and project his certain help into the future. Tell how God has answered your prayers.

Does your church have natural word-of-mouth recognition in its ministry area? If not, then you will need to develop a strategy to help improve your image in the community.

9

How Do You Say Hello?

There is an old saying that you never have a second chance to make a first impression. How do you say hello to first-time visitors to your church? One effective way is to provide a quality *first-impression piece*—a brochure that is given to new people as a way to briefly inform them about your church.

Important Preliminaries

Before you contact a graphic artist or even write a word of copy for your brochure, write out answers to the following questions.

1. What is the purpose of your church?
2. What makes your church unique in contrast to other churches in your area?
3. What are some benefits that people can expect to receive from attending your church?
4. What are new members saying about your church? A way to find out is to interview people.

5. Who is the primary audience that you hope to reach with this advertising piece—families, youth, elderly, singles, a particular ethnic group?
6. What do you want the reader to know, think, feel, and do after reading your first-impression piece?
7. What resources do you have available for producing this piece? Resources include budget, time, people who can help, and equipment. You also must consider who should be the final authority for the approval of your brochure.

The answers to these questions will help you determine what to include in your brochure and how to word it.

Cover

Typically four out of five readers will look only at the first page of a brochure. It must be designed to catch the attention of as many readers as possible, so they will read the inside as well.

A cover should include:

- A photo or drawing that illustrates your purpose or mission. Use pictures of people *not* buildings.
- A title that implies a benefit. For example, "New Hope: The Friendly Church That Cares" implies that there is hope, friendship, and concern at that church. Or "Catch the Spirit of New Life at Community Presbyterian Church," which implies an exciting new approach to life.
- A church logo that is up to date in design. Ask an art or print professional to review your logo and make suggestions about modernizing it. Consider the design, color, and clarity of its meaning.
- A statement that notes some benefits of your church. Why would anyone want to come? What benefits will they receive by attending your church? For example, "At Hope

Church you'll make new friends, discover answers to life's hard questions, and learn to live life to the fullest."

Body

The main part of your first-impression piece should give people an overview of your church. Resist the desire to say everything. Remember that this is just a *first*-impression piece. If it does its job, there will be further opportunities to tell more of your story to the people who begin attending your church. The copy should be readable, with loosely set text, written in the everyday language of the readers.

The body will include *some* of the following. You will need to decide which items are the most important for your target audience.

- Photos that depict church activities and a cross section of your membership.
- Statements about the benefits of attending your church.
- Special features of your church.
- A short biography or sketch of your senior pastor or pastors along with staff photos and descriptions of their responsibilities.
- Testimonials from various people in your church along with their photos if possible.
- A statement of your church's purpose or mission written in everyday language. Resist the desire to say or define your purpose in too much detail. Twenty-five words or less is best.
- A simple map showing your church's location.
- An overview sketch of your church facilities (this is essential for larger churches with complex facilities).
- A brief description of programs and activities for every age group.

- Photos of your congregation participating in worship and other activities.
- Stories of how people in your church are being served.
- Photos and descriptions of your church's service to the community at large.
- A short article on how to get involved.
- A brief schedule of activities.
- An invitation to visit.
- Offers of professional help or service.

Backside or Mailing Panel

Design your first-impression piece so that it may be used in a variety of ways. It should be sized so that it fits into a standard business envelope and should include a mailing panel so that it can also be mailed without an envelope.

Be sure the following information is in your brochure.

- Your church's name, complete address, and phone number. Include postal codes and area codes.
- The times of your various programs and their location.
- An indication of mailing class (important if mailing is to be bulk rate; contact your post office's bulk mail room for information).
- An indicia (postage marking) on the mailing panel and a return address. Remember to get your local postmaster's approval of the mailing panel and format if using a self-mailer.

Design and Printing

Since you want this piece to make a positive first impression on the people who read it, it is best to:

- Get outside help from freelance art, copywriting, market-ing, and printing professionals.
- Solicit bids from several printers.
- Establish a rapport with your designer and printer.
- Select quality paper, popular colors, and up-to-date type-faces.

Your first-impression piece should be designed and writ-ten with unchurched people in mind. It should be attractive and usable in a variety of situations. Because a well-designed first-impression piece is the cornerstone of a church adver-tising plan, you will want to invest time and thought into its development.

PART 4

PEOPLE FLOW

10

IS YOUR CHURCH FRIENDLY?

If you were to survey churches and ask them what their strengths are, almost everyone would say, "We're a friendly church." However, if you were to survey the visitors who attend those same churches, you might find a totally opposite perception.

People who are regular attendees of a church look at the issue of friendliness from the inside out. From their perspective, they are experiencing a friendly atmosphere. They know other people and other people know them. When they have a personal need, other people take notice and respond with appropriate action.

Guests to a church view the issue of friendliness from the outside in. From their perspective, they are experiencing a totally new atmosphere. They may not know other people, and other people may not know them. If they have needs, they are rarely noticed, let alone responded to with appropriate action.

Instinctively we expect churches to be friendly places. Some church growth studies have even found a direct correlation between friendliness and potential growth. The friendlier a church is the greater its potential for growth. The less friendly it is the lower its potential for growth.

How then do we build a church that is friendly to newcomers? The following are several practical guidelines that you can begin using right away.

The Best Attitude

Once while walking through a local shopping center, I noticed a sign in a store window that read: "Hiring. Only friendly people need apply." The owners of that store obviously knew that customers appreciate a friendly attitude and were determined to hire only friendly people.

In a similar way visitors to your church notice immediately the prevailing attitude. In fact most visitors will make a judgment about your church within thirty seconds of their entering the front door.

If you want to be a friendly church, I suggest you recruit friendly ushers, greeters, and parking attendants who will project enthusiasm, courtesy, and pride to your guests.

The Best Communication

As a church consultant, I visit several churches for the first time every year. One of my favorite techniques is to station myself in a busy part of the auditorium or foyer to see how many people speak to me. Many times people walk toward me, our eyes meet, and then they look toward the floor and walk on by.

If this is happening in your church, it has the effect of making your guests feel like nonpersons. They will not perceive you as a friendly church.

If you want to be a friendly church, I suggest you teach your regular attendees to follow the "ten-foot rule" and the "just-say-hi policy." Whenever they come within ten feet of a person they don't know, they should just say hi.

The Best Service

Recently I visited a rather large church in Southern California. As my wife and I stepped up on the curb to enter the front door, a lady greeted us by saying, "Hi! Is this your first time with us?" After we answered yes, she introduced herself, asked our names, and walked with us into the building to a welcome center.

At the welcome center she introduced us by name to the person at the desk who immediately offered help and gave us directions to important areas of the church, such as the restrooms and the auditorium.

As we were about to finish our conversation at the welcome center, an usher walked up, and the person behind the desk introduced us by name to him. He then led us to our seats in the auditorium.

In just a few minutes we had been introduced to several very friendly people, had our names mentioned three times, and were given all the initial information we needed.

While you may not wish to follow this church's exact procedure, if you want to be a friendly church, I suggest you adopt the three principles they used:

- Approach new people promptly.
- Offer help and information.
- Introduce visitors by name to others.

The Best Welcome

I was very tired. As I sat down in the auditorium, my only desire was to be left alone to worship. To my dismay the pastor asked all visitors to stand. Then one by one he went around the room asking each of us to introduce ourselves and to give a short word of greeting to the congregation. Even though I'm a seasoned churchgoer, it was more than embarrassing. It put me on the spot, and I wondered how others felt.

In today's society it is good to welcome guests as a group from the pulpit but not to have them stand to be recognized. Give guests freedom to relax and enjoy the worship service. Whatever you do, take great pains not to embarrass the newcomer.

The Best Parking

In our age of the automobile, three things continue to be true about most people. First, people don't like to walk more than one block to church. Second, people will drive around for several minutes to find a parking place close to the entrance. Third, if they don't find a parking space where they want it, they will drive on by without stopping.

If you want to be a friendly church, I suggest you reserve approximately 5 percent of your parking places for guests as close to your main entrance as possible. And clearly mark them for first- or second-time guests.

The Best Seats

The most popular seats on an airplane are the aisle seats, because people like to have a sense of openness and don't like feeling trapped. Likewise church guests prefer the aisle seats and the seats in the rear of the auditorium. Unfortunately, those are the places most regular attendees like to sit!

If you want to be a friendly church, reserve the aisle seats and the rear seats for guests. Make sure the ushers understand where guests prefer to sit, and encourage your regular attenders to sit in the middle of longer rows and closer to the front.

The Best Time

At the end of one church service the pastor gave the closing benediction and then said to the audience: "Remember the five-minute rule." This intrigued me since I had never heard of a five-minute rule.

I later found out that the people of that church had been instructed to speak to guests during the first five minutes following each worship service. As I mentioned in an earlier chapter, this meant that they were not to do any church business or talk to their friends until five minutes had elapsed.

If you want to be a friendly church, I suggest you and your regular attenders reserve the first five minutes following every worship service for greeting your guests.

Albert Einstein was once asked what he considered to be the most important question in the world. He replied, "Is the universe a friendly place?" Guests who visit a church are asking a similar question—"Is this church a friendly place?" What do they conclude when they visit your church?

11

WHAT GUESTS SEE

To honestly appreciate the new person's experience when attending your church for the first time, you need to set aside your "insider" understanding and think like an "outsider." A good way to do so is to list the key experiences of guests to your church. Then walk through each one with "guest eyes," attempting to understand how your guests would feel.

There are, of course, many moments of engagement when a guest enters your church. Newcomers to every church face the ten that follow. Think through each one and describe what happens now and what should happen when a guest experiences each one at your church.

Driving up to the church building. Is the landscaping around your church well kept? Is the parking lot nicely paved and clear of debris? Are the exterior walls and windows of the building attractive? Are there parking spaces clearly marked for guests?

Walking up to the front door. Are there warm and friendly people greeting guests before they enter the building? Is the entrance clearly marked? Does the entrance present an inviting look that says, "Please, come in"?

Entering the front door. Are the sounds that guests hear on entering the building inviting? Is there a pleasant smell? Does the decor seem attractive and welcoming? Is it clear where they should go? Are there people available to answer questions and give assistance?

Meeting people. Are church members outgoing and approachable? Do they appear to be accepting of newcomers? Do they exhibit an honest friendliness without seeming mushy or overbearing?

Experiencing ministries and services. Is the child care area clean, bright, and open? Are the restrooms clean and free of unpleasant odors? Are classrooms nicely decorated?

Meeting ushers and entering the sanctuary. Do ushers smile and make an effort to be friendly? Is the atmosphere of the worship area vibrant and happy? Is there room to sit without being crowded? Are guests welcomed graciously and treated with respect?

Participating in the worship service. Is the order of the worship service explained and easy for guests to follow? Are the songs ones that newcomers can sing? Are the words of the songs available to them? Do newcomers leave the service wishing it had been longer or shorter? Do guests feel at ease and comfortable?

Exiting the worship service. Do guests find a friendly atmosphere when leaving the worship area? Do people around them take time to greet them? Are they invited to a refreshment table to talk and meet others from the church?

Future contacts. Are guests contacted personally within forty-eight hours of their first visit to your church? Do you thank them for their attendance? Do you invite them back? Do you ask for their evaluation of your church? Do you in some way surprise guests with an extra measure of service beyond what they expect?

Ongoing contacts. Are guests put on your mailing list for appropriate future contact? Do guests receive a church newsletter on a regular basis? Do you mail them informational brochures describing ministries they might find interesting? Do you call them to extend a personal invitation to special events?

12

PATHWAYS OF BELONGING

A number of years ago I accepted a new job at a company that was good at welcoming its new employees. When I arrived at my new place of employment, I was met warmly at the reception desk by the vice president of the company who personally escorted me to my office. He told me to take about thirty minutes to get settled, put a few things in my desk, and then meet him in his office.

When I went to his office, he proceeded to take me on a walking tour of the entire facility. Along the way he introduced me to every employee from management to the mailroom personnel. He answered any questions that I asked and generally gave me a superb introduction to the company.

We went to lunch with the president and two additional vice presidents of the company. During lunch they casually shared their basic values and philosophies of work. My entire first day was given to meeting people and getting acquainted with the company. Nothing about my particular job assignment was even mentioned until the second day.

What had taken place on my first day on the job was what should take place in every company . . . and church. The vice president who led me throughout the day was building pathways of belonging for me. Churches should do the same by building pathways of belonging for their guests.

Seven Pathways

Pathways of belonging are strategically designed ministries that assist new people in gaining a sense of being part of a church. There are, of course, many pathways of belonging. Here are seven that churches have found to be effective:

1. *Staff reception.* Set aside a room in the church where guests can come for light refreshments and to meet the pastor or pastoral staff. In smaller churches a staff reception may be offered once a month, while in larger churches it could be a regular Sunday morning event. Extend an invitation from the pulpit, in the program, and through greeters and others who meet guests during the morning. Design the staff reception to give new people an initial acquaintance with the leaders of the church.

2. *Pastor's dessert.* The purpose of the pastor's dessert is to welcome those who have attended the church a minimum of three times. The pastor reserves one night a month to invite guests to his home. Mail a nicely printed invitation, similar to a wedding invitation, to each person who has been identified as visiting at least three times. Encourage guests to RSVP and to dress casually. Use the dessert to help guests build friendships with the staff and each other.

3. *Orientation class.* An orientation class introduces people to your church's purpose, vision, goals, and values. In small churches, the pastor will teach this class, but in larger ones a staff member can do the job. Since people today are not necessarily interested in church membership, it's good not to name the class a "new members'

class." Find a name that communicates a different value, such as "Meet Hope Community Church" or "How to Belong." Churches find that four to six hours of class time is enough to get the job done.

4. *Small groups.* People gain ownership in a church as they make friends and participate in a class or group. A good way to facilitate this is to extend the orientation class into a small group. Guests may develop beginning friendships in your orientation class that they will want to continue once the class concludes. Ask the orientation class participants if they would enjoy continuing on together as a small group, meeting on an evening or Sunday morning. If they desire to continue meeting together, you will have established a new group and further assisted the new people in gaining ownership in your church.

5. *Dinner eights.* Invite a new couple or individual to alternate hosting a meal at their home with two or three other couples or individuals. The purpose of the meals is to get to know each other better. Once each month for three or four months, alternate the group from one home to another for a meal. In a smaller church, it often works well to have the pastor's family be one of the couples along with the new family and others who regularly attend the church. This helps the new family get to know church members and feel like they are a part of the church. When it is possible, it is always best for groups to be formed of people with similar interests.

6. *New believers' class.* There will be some new people who need teaching in the basic doctrines of your church and the Christian faith. Thus a new believers' class is another pathway some people need to follow. The purpose of this class is to teach about the basics of salvation and other beginning aspects of being a disciple of Jesus Christ. This class may also serve to explain the church's distinctives. Invite newcomers to this class both publicly and privately.

7. *Placement interview.* Some new people may have taken the initiative to become involved in a ministry on their

own. For those who have not, a leader should schedule an interview to discover their gifts, talents, previous experience, and ministry desires. Following the interview, a ministry counselor from your church can offer several possibilities of ministry and put the new person in touch with the director of the ministries they are interested in pursuing. A concerted effort to interview and place new people will pay rich dividends. New people are the easiest to recruit since they come into your church with a sense of excitement and a willingness to serve.

Questions to Answer

As you build pathways of belonging for the new people coming into your church, think through the following questions:

1. What pathways are available now that assist people in becoming established in your church?
2. What pathways are missing?
3. What pathways do you need to begin building this next year?

When you answer these questions carefully and then follow them up with action, you'll discover that people find their way into your church much more often than they used to.

PART 5

ASSIMILATION

13

ASSIMILATING NEWCOMERS

Churches across the United States have found that assimilation of newcomers is a primary concern. In recent years the insights and ideas that work to effectively bond newcomers to a church have changed.

Ten Important Percentages

Sixty Percent with Little Understanding of Church

In today's world only 40 percent of our guests come from a sister church or one with a similar background. That means that 60 percent come with little or no understanding of our church. Just a little more than forty years ago, approximately 90 percent of a church's guests came from the same denominational background. This meant that they already understood the church's theology, order of worship, music, values, and culture. Such inherent knowledge allowed them to feel comfortable and at ease in the new church, and this made assimilating new members relatively easy.

Now, with more than half of our guests coming with no church background or from one that is quite different, it is a new story. Many newcomers will have little knowledge about the church and will be unfamiliar with the worship format. They do not know when to stand, sit, or kneel. Others do not know our songs, language, and religious jargon. Because of their unfamiliarity with the church, assimilation is more difficult and takes strategic planning.

Fifty Percent Fewer People

With the improvements in automobiles and roads following World War II, Americans' love affair with the car grew even stronger than it already was. At that time families fit into the "breadwinner and homemaker" nuclear family format of father, mother, and 2.2 children. A pastor looking out his office window in the early fifties would have counted three or four people in every car driving into the church parking lot.

Today a pastor viewing cars out the same window will most often see only one or two people in each car (roughly 50 percent fewer people per car). Today each family unit is about half the size and each car brings about 50 percent fewer people to church. Because fewer people are visiting our church, each guest is more valuable and we must be more effective in our assimilation of them.

Ten Percent Leave Each Year

People stayed longer in churches of the early 1950s. The best guess is that in those times churches lost only about 5 percent of their people each year. Family units were still intact; neighborhoods and mutual networks of friendships were fairly strong. The general culture supported a friendliness that benefited churches, and a natural openness provided a friendly welcome to all who came. This, coupled with the tendency of people to remain in the same geographical area and on the same job for a lifetime, made concerns about assimilating people less of an issue.

Today churches lose about 10 percent of their worshipers each year (some many more). In our mobile society people move three to six times, with some moving up to twenty times, in their lifetime. Add to this the fracturing of the family, the breakdown of natural networks of friendships, the general cautiousness of people, and we can understand why it is more of a challenge to assimilate people into our churches today.

Sixteen Percent of First-Time Guests

Research completed in the late 1980s found that a church must keep about 16 percent of its first-time guests to experience a minimal growth rate of 5 percent a year. Rapidly growing churches assimilate 25 to 30 percent of their first-time guests. Declining churches keep only about 5 to 8 percent of their first-time guests. By using the average of 16 percent, we can calculate the number of guests a church needs to grow. As an example, a church that wants to assimilate fifty new members this year will need to have a minimum of three hundred guests attend its worship services during the year.

Eighty-Five Percent of Returning Guests

The same research revealed the crucial importance of getting guests to return for a second visit. A church keeps about 85 percent of its guests who come back for a second visit the week after their first visit. This points out the importance of being gracious hosts the first time so that guests will feel encouraged to return. Our assimilation strategy for first-time guests should focus on getting them to visit a second time.

Instinctively we expect churches to be friendly places. Research studies completed by Dr. Win Arn in the mid-1980s found a direct correlation between friendliness and potential growth. In short, he found that friendly churches were more effective at assimilation while less friendly churches assimilated fewer people.

Twenty Percent New Groups

While many churches find they have a large number of classes and groups, most still find it difficult to assimilate newcomers into the life of their fellowship. This is because classes and groups tend to close to the addition of new people within two years. If most of a church's classes and groups were started several years ago, they will not be open to new members. Churches that effectively assimilate newcomers into the life of their church make it a point to begin new classes and groups on a regular time schedule so that a minimum of 20 percent of them are less than two years old.

Fifty Percent in Small Groups

As a general rule, most churches that stress small-group ministry find it fairly easy to involve 50 percent of their adults in their cell groups. A few churches that make small groups the major emphasis of their assimilation strategy often recruit 60–75 percent of their adults into groups.

Ninety Percent Remain Loyal

Newcomers enter a church looking for three key elements: friends, a place to belong, and a ministry. Is it any wonder that classes and small groups are often attractive places to assimilate new people? It is in these small gatherings that we usually develop loving friendships, a group identity, and quite often a place of service. As many as 90 percent of all newcomers who join a small group remain loyal to the church.

Seventy-Five Percent Assimilate Quickly

Seventy-five percent of those who become active in a church do so within six to twelve months of first attending. In most cases it is a mistake to encourage newcomers to sit on the sidelines for a year or two before getting involved in a ministry. After sitting for that length of time, quite a few new people never transition into Christian service. Churches hoping to assimilate new people for the long haul find it wiser to recruit and involve newcomers in a ministry within three to six months of their first visit.

Twenty-One Percent in Neighborhood Groups

Even though crime rates are rising, people are not arming themselves. Instead of buying guns for protection, 21 percent of Americans have already joined neighborhood watch groups. Reportedly another 14 percent are thinking of doing so. The most popular action for those living in high-crime areas is to reach out to others and make connections. Small relational groups are still attractive ways to assimilate the average person if they provide a sense of purpose, a friendly atmosphere, and a supportive environment.

Increasing Assimilation

How does your church match up against these percentages? What do you need to begin doing this year that will help you be more effective in assimilating newcomers into the fellowship of your church? Church leaders understand that effective follow-up of guests is an important ingredient to their church's growth mix. While there is no one assimilation strategy that works in every church, the following are concepts that have proven to work more effectively than others.

> *Enhance your friendliness.* Growing churches generate a friendly environment. To create a friendly atmosphere, focus your attention on the newcomer who is visiting your worship services.
>
> *Hire an assimilation pastor.* The job description of an assimilation pastor includes responsibility for developing an overall assimilation plan that includes some of the following elements.
> * follow-up of all guests

- tracking attendance at worship services
- recruiting and training of ushers, greeters, and parking attendants
- overseeing the welcome center and refreshment table
- organizing the newcomers' classes

Develop a welcome center. Establishing a welcome center is an excellent way to tell your guests that your church cares about them. Place the welcome center in a high-traffic area of the church where new people are likely to see it and staff it with friendly people who find it easy to talk to strangers. Provide information sheets on all the ministries offered by your church. If your church has several entrances, provide several small welcome centers in each traffic area.

Use a hospitality table. The well-planned use of a hospitality table provides a way to greet visitors in a comfortable setting. When people have a cup of coffee or juice in one hand and a donut in the other, it relaxes them, making it much easier to talk with them. Locate the hospitality table where newcomers will walk by it. Recruit friendly people to be hosts and encourage your greeters to hang around it to meet newcomers. Occasionally change the location of the table and put different colored tablecloths on it so that people notice it.

Train hosts and greeters. The main goal of a greeter is to extend a warm welcome to anyone who is attending your church, especially the newcomers, and to treat them as guests. To do this, one church identified seven objectives for their greeters:

Generate a comfortable atmosphere.
Respect a person's anonymity.
Extend a hand of friendship.
Express your genuine interest.
Treat others as the Lord would.
Encourage them to come back.
Request to meet their needs.

Track participation. While leaders are not called by God to be truant officers, they are expected to shepherd the church of God (1 Peter 5:2) and one way to do that is to track participation. Most churches request guests to complete a registration card or fill in a friendship pad. The least effective way to register guests is a registration book located near the entry of the church.

Develop a specific process. Organize a process for assimilating newcomers by making a chart showing the steps your church will use to welcome, follow up, invite back, and care for newcomers.

14

GETTING READY FOR COMPANY

Whenever company is coming over to our house we go through a regular ritual of "getting ready for company." For us this involves such things as cleaning the bathrooms, emptying the trash, vacuuming the floor, dusting the counters, and, most important, changing the cat litter boxes.

All our effort is expended in preparation for our guests. We want our house to look the best it can and we spare no amount of effort to see that it is ready. No doubt you can identify with this ritual.

In a similar way, growing churches spend a significant amount of time getting ready for their company—newcomers to their church. They know that:

- *It takes guests to grow.* No church grows unless guests visit. As a general rule of thumb a church needs to average between 4 and 5 percent of its worship attendance as first-time guests before significant growth occurs.

- *Some guests must return.* Growing churches create an atmosphere to which guests want to return for another visit. As a general rule of thumb at least two out of every ten first-time guests must return a second time for a church to experience numerical growth.
- *Guests make quick decisions.* Most guests form an early opinion of a church as they drive into the parking lot and within thirty seconds of entering the front door. If their first opinion is negative, it may be difficult to change their mind.

Because of these realities, a church must consciously prepare for its guests. The following are seven key areas to address.

Beautify Your Property

Guests begin forming an opinion about a church as they drive toward it. They notice the landscaping, the parking lot, the color of the buildings, and the general appearance of the entire church property.

To get ready for company:

- Repaint the exterior every three to five years.
- Redecorate the interior every five years to keep the colors, styles, and overall look up to date.
- Maintain landscaping through a weekly lawn care service.
- Hire a professional landscaping firm to review the exterior look every three years.
- Clean the entire church weekly.
- Replace carpet and drapes every five to ten years.

Upgrade Your Child Care

With the new generation of children coming to our churches, there are parents who are astute child-care shoppers. Parents expect a church's nursery to be comparable to their baby's room at home. They look for a church nursery to provide the same quality care they would find at the best day care centers.

To get ready for company:

- Redecorate the nursery every other year.
- Sanitize the nursery each week.
- Keep the ratio of workers to children at 1:3.
- Provide a hazard-free environment.
- Retrain all nursery workers yearly.
- Maintain the same workers for familiarity.

For more on providing the best child care, see chapter 26.

Give People Directions

The number one question asked at places like Disneyland is "Where are the restrooms?" Guests in your church also need directions to key areas, such as restrooms, auditorium, and nursery.

To get ready for company:

- Prepare a one-page map showing all the important locations for newcomers.
- Provide leaflets describing each major area of ministry, their locations, and whom to contact for further information.
- Install clear directional signs at eye level pointing the way to key areas of the church.
- Train hosts to greet and direct newcomers to important areas.

Welcome Guests Graciously

Enter the door of a Wal-Mart store, and you will be greeted by a friendly person who offers you a shopping cart. Wal-Mart understands the need to greet guests graciously, and their success has prompted competitors to follow suit.

To get ready for company:

- Give a positive welcome to people driving into the parking lot through the use of parking attendants.
- Extend a warm greeting to new guests as they approach the church building through trained greeters.
- Provide relevant information about the church with an attractive and accessible information table or welcome center.
- Establish meaningful connections between new guests and the people of the church by introducing members to guests.
- Provide refreshments for guests before and after the worship service at a hospitality table.
- Ensure the comfortable seating of guests during the service with friendly ushers.

Enhance the Worship Service

People in our society are attuned to well-planned and well-executed programs. While a worship service is certainly more than a mere performance, it needs to be done well to get most guests to return a second and third time.

To get ready for company:

- Build a worship service around one theme.
- Allow for participation by worshipers.
- Create a sense of flow in the service.
- Speed up the pace.
- Eliminate dead time.
- Use variety.

Preach Relational Messages

Blended families; single-parent families; codependency relationships; and physical, mental, sexual, and substance abuse have created hurting people. Guests visit a church not to be scolded but to be uplifted.

To get ready for company:

- Understand the felt needs of people.
- Provide biblical answers to people's felt needs.
- Illustrate messages from today's life and times.
- Tell stories of real people who have experienced similar needs and found answers in Christ.
- Remove physical obstacles that block the congregation's view, such as modesty rails, large pulpits, and furniture.
- Preach without notes so you can maintain eye contact with the audience.
- Share your own story.

Follow Up Appropriately

Traditionally, when guests attended a church, they received a letter from the pastor and an immediate visit to their home by a visitation team. Today with the rise of crime and the cocooning of people in their homes, it's a whole new ball game.

To get ready for company:

- Express your friendship through a personal phone call within two days of the visit to the church.
- Thank each guest with a personal letter, card, or e-mail message during the week.
- Inform guests of upcoming events and items of interest through a regular newsletter.
- Ask all third-time guests to a by-invitation-only dessert hosted by the senior pastor.

15

Visitor Follow-Up That Works!

Church leaders understand that effective follow-up of visitors is an important ingredient to their church's growth mix. Traditionally churches have accomplished visitor follow-up through a personal visit in the new person's home by a pastor or calling team. Today many churches are finding that this method is no longer as effective as it used to be.

General Principles

Here are some general principles to follow when doing visitor follow-up. People seem to be most responsive when they receive:

- *A friendly contact.* Offer your friendship. Care should be taken not to offend new people in any way.
- *A personal contact.* Focus on the visitor's interests and needs that are ascertained from the initial contact. Nothing

takes the place of a personal touch in our high tech–high touch age, no matter how it is accomplished.

- *A prompt contact.* Contact visitors within twenty-four hours. The longer the time between their visit and a contact the less effective the contact will be.
- *A nonthreatening contact.* Put the visitor at ease. People have a natural uneasiness around new places and people.
- *A continual contact.* See follow-up as a process not an event. A one-time contact is not enough to be effective in our present environment.

Some Insights

Follow up second-time visitors. The most effective retention of visitors occurs when follow-up is focused on second-time visitors. Recent church growth studies have found that the average church in the United States keeps 16 percent of all first-time visitors. In contrast, the average church keeps 85 percent of its second-time visitors!

Focus on prospects. The most effective retention of visitors occurs when follow-up is focused on prospects. Visitors come in two types—suspects and prospects. Suspects are visitors who appear to be interested in Christ and the church but are actually just looking and probably don't intend to stay. Prospects are people who are sincerely interested in Christ and the church.

In general, first-time visitors are suspects. They may be interested in the Lord. They may be interested in the church but, then again, maybe not.

Visitors who return for additional visits are the prospects. By attending your church again, they are in effect saying that they liked what they found the first time. They are back for a closer look.

Build relationships. The most effective retention of visitors occurs when follow-up is focused on building relationships.

Many churches use an institutional approach to follow-up. They focus on what the church needs rather than on caring for the visitor. It is important for visitors to perceive that the church is interested in them and their needs.

Focus on the visitor's expectations. The most effective retention of visitors occurs when follow-up is focused on the expectations of visitors. Today's visitors want their attendance acknowledged, but they do not expect a visit from the pastor. Churches located in cities, in high-tech and crime-ridden areas, will find that people do not want someone showing up on their doorstep without an appointment. Non-Christians and those who find the church threatening wish to remain somewhat anonymous—but not ignored.

A Four-Step Plan

This four-step plan for following up on visitors assumes that your church has a way to attract visitors, get their names and addresses, and know when they have returned for second, third, and fourth visits.

Step One: Acknowledgment

The week following the visitor's *first* visit to your church:

Call the visitor. A person with a friendly phone voice should call the visitor. Shut-ins or elderly people may find this a place for ministry. Call Sunday afternoon if possible and no later than Monday evening. Thank the person for attending, and interview him or her for perceptions of your church. (Note: A sample phone interview is available. Please send a self-addressed, stamped envelope to the McIntosh Church Growth Network. See address at end of book.)

Send a letter. In the letter, signed by the senior pastor, thank the visitor for attending, list the times of your services, and offer general help.

Place visitor's name on church mailing list. Develop a general mailing list for all potential contacts and a prime list for people who are regular attenders. Mail brochures, church newsletters, and general information to people on the general mailing list.

Step Two: Appointment

The week following the visitor's *second* visit to your church:

Call for an appointment. In most cases it is unwise to show up at the door unexpectedly. Call the visitor and ask for an appointment (nine out of ten people will refuse). If the person says yes, schedule the appointment. If he or she says no, ask if you could send further information concerning your church.

Make a personal visit. If the visitor seems resistant to your offer to come to his or her home, make a lunch appointment and meet in a conveniently located restaurant. Or invite visitors to your home after church or take them to breakfast before church.

Mail further information. Develop a detailed information piece on your church. This should be different from the one mailed after the first visit and should provide additional details about your church.

Step Three: Enhancement

The week following the visitor's *third* visit to your church:

Mail a card. A postcard lets the visitor know that the church is aware of their third visit. A greeting card also works well.

Arrange a personal contact. Someone in the church who has similar interests should make a follow-up phone call or visit and may be able to meet some of the guest's needs. For example, if the visitor has expressed an interest in crafts, sports, or a hobby, have someone who has similar interests give him or her a call.

Step Four: Commitment

The week immediately following the visitor's *fourth* visit to your church:

Ask for modest commitment. You might say, "We've noticed you have been attending on a regular basis. Would you like your name placed in our directory?" (This assumes you have a directory that can be changed once every three months. Pictorial directories are not good for this.)

Invite the visitor to an orientation class. If the person is a non-Christian or new believer, invite him or her to a new believers' class for orientation to the Christian faith. If the person is a Christian, invite him or her to a new members' class for orientation to your church.

By following the above plan, you will contact the visitor up to eight times in a four-week period. These recurring contacts will build a relationship that will lead to many more than 16 percent of your first-time visitors remaining as active worshipers. Churches that have used a similar plan are often able to retain nearly 25 percent of their first-time visitors.

PART 6

WORSHIP

16

CELEBRATIVE WORSHIP SERVICES

Quick! Name the ministry that does the most to help a church grow. If you're like most people, you've named the celebrative worship service. But what exactly is a celebrative worship service? How do we create one? What does it take to make a worship service effective?

Enthusiastic Worship

Clearly defining a celebrative worship service is difficult, yet we all seem to know one when we experience it. From a practical point of view, worship is celebrative when:

- *People attend.* Celebrative services attract people who come because they want to rather than because they have to.
- *People bring friends.* Celebrative services not only attract people but also encourage worshipers to bring their friends.

- *People participate.* Celebrative services create an environment where singing, giving, praying, and other aspects of worship are entered into with enthusiasm.
- *People listen.* Celebrative services hold the attention of worshipers throughout the entire time of worship.
- *People grow.* Celebrative services challenge individuals to make biblical decisions that affect their daily living.

After observing many different celebrative worship services, I have come up with the following insights.

Celebrative worship services hold people's attention. Church leaders often say, "We don't want to entertain people." In reality what they mean is "We don't want to amuse people." *Amusement* means to idle away time, to divert attention. In contrast, *entertainment* means to hold the attention of, to hold in mind. While worship services should not amuse, they should obviously hold the attention of people who participate.

Celebrative worship services communicate to the whole person. Effective worship services take seriously the mental, spiritual, relational, and emotional nature of worshipers. Unfortunately, many worship services tend to focus primarily on the mind, without seriously speaking to the whole person. While worship services should challenge people mentally, to be truly celebrative they must also speak to the emotions, spirit, and heart of the worshipers.

Celebrative worship services excite those who attend. Walk into some worship services and you can feel the enthusiasm in the air. It is hard to define this feeling, yet we instinctively know celebrative services have it and others do not. While we certainly don't want to create a false enthusiasm, if worshipers experience high energy, they will likely view the service as celebrative. If the energy level is low, they may never return.

Enhancing Worship

The following six ideas will help you create a more exciting and celebrative worship service that will hold your people's attention.

Build around one theme. Celebrative worship services have a sense of unity that is best achieved by building the entire service around one basic theme. *To enhance your worship services*, identify the broad theme you wish to communicate to your audience. Select and use music that fits your theme. Be sure to relate your introductions, transitional comments, and even your announcements to the theme.

Plan for participation. Celebrative worship services keep people alert by involving them in meaningful ways throughout the service. *To enhance your worship services*, build in ways for people to participate. Allow for singing, clapping, standing, shaking hands, filling in blanks in a study guide, praying, hugging, talking, laughing, crying, and other audience participation.

Develop a sense of flow. Celebrative worship services lead people along so that they sense a clear flow or progression in the service. *To enhance your worship services*, think through how each part of the service relates to the whole. Sporadic or disconnected components will cause people to become distracted and disinterested.

Speed up the pace. Celebrative worship services move along quickly enough to keep people's attention focused on the service. *To enhance your worship services*, vary the pace of the music by using upbeat celebrative tempos as well as slower reflective tempos. The music should not drag and should encourage worship.

Eliminate dead time. Celebrative worship services move quickly between various parts of the service, allowing for little dead time when people may become inattentive. *To enhance your worship services*, develop good transitions between the various elements of the worship service. All movement between people and elements of worship should take place quickly and smoothly.

Use variety. Celebrative worship services use a variety of worship elements to maintain everyone's interest and enjoyment. *To enhance your worship services*, include a variety of elements, such as drama, interviews, video, a message, the greeting of one another, Scripture reading, an offering, and music.

Celebrative worship services start with advanced planning. So:

- Recruit a worship team to help develop creative services.
- Plan your worship services four to six weeks ahead of time.
- Use the six ideas above to enhance your worship services.

17

MULTIPLE WORSHIP SERVICES

One of the trends of growing churches today is their multiple worship services. While adding a second service is not a new idea, some churches are now adding three, four, and even five services on nights not normally used for worship in Protestant churches.

The Reasoning

In this new century, it is likely that at least 50 percent of all churches will seriously consider the addition of at least one new worship service. It is important for churches to consider why they should add a service before they worry about when and how to do it.

There are seven major reasons churches give for adding an additional service. In general, multiple worship services:

Provide options. The one-size-fits-all worship service is quickly becoming a thing of the past. From gas stations to hamburger stands to varieties of cereal in a supermarket, everywhere there are choices in our society. Adding a new worship service is one way to provide choices in church ministry.

Expand space. In today's environment land purchases and facility development are often not affordable options for many congregations. Multiple services allow a church to use its present facility two or more times without having to enter into an expensive building program.

Allow for growth. An overcrowded auditorium actually discourages numerical growth. Studies of churches that have gone from one worship service to two have found that most (80 percent) experience between 15 and 20 percent growth in overall worship attendance. (See chapter 38 for more information on this phenomenon.)

Increase faith. Churches with a single service essentially place their emphasis on present members. Churches that offer more than one worship service tend to place an emphasis on reaching newer members, which takes vision and faith.

Enlarge ministry. There is a limit to how many people can minister in a single worship service. By adding additional services, a church nearly doubles the ministry roles and tasks in which people can become involved. And as a rule of thumb, for every person who has a ministry, another three will attend the service with them.

Reach new people. The singular character of one worship service as to style and time generally attracts only one kind of person. By adding an additional service with a different time and style, new people are attracted who might not normally attend.

Keep people happy. The changing preferences of people regarding such things as music, dress, and time are too complex to address in one worship service. Multiple services allow for a church to zero in on varied preferences.

The Timing

To be most successful, it is best to add an additional service when the growth momentum is rising, the morale is high, and the timing is right.

Rising Momentum

One of the mistakes churches often make is adding a new service when it is too late. The key is to add an additional service as the growth momentum is heading upward not after it has peaked and is going down.

By charting an accurate record of worship attendance on a graph, a church will be able to tell when the growth momentum is rising. As worship attendance nears 80 percent capacity, plans should be made to add another service. Then the new service should be added as attendance moves into and through 90 percent capacity.

High Morale

Adding an additional service is a step of faith. If a church is going through a period of discouragement or is experiencing conflict, it should resolve the issues before moving to multiple services.

While going to an additional worship service is an exciting option, doing so will not revive a dying or demoralized congregation. Ideally, adding an additional service should be the natural result of growth—both spiritual and numerical.

Right Moment

Many attempts to add services fail simply due to wrong timing. A new service stands the best chance of succeeding when it is added during the normal growth periods of the church year.

The best time to add an additional service is in the early fall

(September or October) or winter (January through March) to take advantage of the regular growth peaks of church attendance. In only rare cases should an additional service be added after Easter and on through the summer months, because attendance tends to go down during these times.

The Major Issues

Any church wishing to begin a new worship service would do well to think through the following issues.

Style of services. The major issue facing many churches is whether the new worship service will be identical to the previous one(s) or a different style. *The key factor* in making this determination is the diversity of the congregation.

Balancing attendance. An issue often overlooked is whether attendance at all services will be balanced. *Key factors* in accomplishing a balanced attendance are the seating capacity of the auditorium, the makeup of the congregation (singles, couples with children, elderly), and general lifestyle characteristics.

Scheduling. The actual time schedule to be used is an issue that can make or break the new service. *Key factors* to consider are the traffic flow (people and automobiles), fellowship needs, and the lifestyles of the attendees.

Child care. One of the most difficult issues to address when adding services is when and how to provide the necessary child care. *Key factors* to consider are the ages of children in your congregation, the expectation of members, and the number of potential child care workers.

Music. Multiple services increase the need for more music personnel. *The key factor* in answering this need is the availability of current and potential music personnel.

Support ministries. Adding a new worship service requires additional support personnel. *The key factor* in providing support ministries is the availability of additional support people, such as ushers and greeters.

18

ADDING
A SECOND SERVICE

Growing churches find that multiple worship services are a good way to meet the needs of people in our fast-paced society. Before adding a service, however, several questions need to be answered.

What Are the Options for Scheduling?

There are three basic approaches to scheduling multiple worship services on Sunday mornings. Most churches find it best to move progressively from one approach to another as they experience growth.

The Sandwich Approach

Worship

Sunday School

Worship

For churches with a traditional schedule of Sunday school followed by morning worship, the easiest transition to multiple services is to use the sandwich approach. This approach simply adds a second worship service before Sunday school, thus sandwiching Sunday school between two worship services.

This approach is the easiest way to begin since it creates the least disruption to the schedule already in place.

The Flip-Flop Approach

Worship/Sunday School

Worship/Sunday School

Churches using the flip-flop approach offer two worship services and two Sunday schools together. Ministry personnel may then flip-flop back and forth between services, working in one and attending another. Likewise, this model gives people who attend one worship service the opportunity to attend the other Sunday school.

The Consecutive Approach

Worship

Worship/Sunday School

Worship/Sunday School

Churches that experience continual growth often add three consecutive worship services on Sunday mornings. Most will offer only two complete Sunday schools with limited child care during the earliest service.

Which Service Will Be Most Popular?

In general, the service that starts between 9:00 and 10:00 AM will be the largest. In the initial stages one service will have about two-thirds of the total attendance and the other one-third.

It is important not to have an empty feeling in any worship service, because people feel uncomfortable in a service where less than 35 percent of the seating is filled. The perception of an empty or full service is based more on the seats available than on the actual size of the room. If possible, remove chairs or pews and widen aisles to make the worship service seem fuller.

Should Services Be Identical?

If the goals for adding an additional worship service are to attract new people, take advantage of people's different gifts, expand opportunities for service, or give people greater options, it is wise to offer a choice of worship styles rather than identical services.

Are Saturday Services a Good Idea?

Some churches find that Thursday, Friday, or Saturday evenings are good times for adding a new worship service. Churches interested in pursuing an evening worship service should be aware that:

- Successful evening worship services are normally a spill-over of an already strong Sunday morning ministry. Do not attempt to start an evening worship service unless attendance at Sunday morning worship services is strong.
- Evening worship services tend to have a more casual and laid-back atmosphere than Sunday morning services.
- Evening worship services often lack the same intensity of Sunday morning services, as worshipers come directly from work or other activities and may be tired.

- Evening worship services are a good option for people who work on weekends and/or prefer to use the weekend for travel or recreational activities.

How Should a Church Proceed?

Consider the following ideas as you develop plans for an additional worship service.

Begin keeping accurate records. Keep track of worship attendance, the number of cars in the parking lot, and the ratio of children to adults in the worship service. (If children participate in part of the worship service before going to their own classes, you will need to add services sooner.) Especially note when worship attendance reaches 80 percent of the seating capacity. This is when you can begin thinking seriously about adding a worship service.

Prepare your leadership. Train church leaders to understand the relationship of seating, parking, and child care to overall growth in worship attendance. Share with them the positive reasons for multiple services. Suggest a strategy for adding services as they are needed.

Educate the congregation. Direct the congregation's attention to the Great Commission. Alert them to the possibility of adding multiple worship services, and solicit comments through surveys and personal contacts. Research people's preference in worship style and times for multiple services.

Set a target date. Develop a strategic plan and communicate to worshipers a possible target date to begin multiple services.

Train additional staff. Consider the number of ministry personnel needed to support the new service. Start recruiting and training additional ushers, musicians, child care workers, Sunday school staff, and worship teams. Look for people who are not serving, and seek to involve them in support roles.

Communicate the change. Inform members who have not been attending, the present congregation, and other potential worshipers about the new service. Use the newspaper, direct mail, and small weekly papers.

Experiment for one year. Promote the new service as an experiment. If possible, conduct the additional worship service for nine to twelve months before conducting a full review.

PART 7

RENEWAL

19

Turning a Church Around

You can't do ministry as usual if you want to turn a declining church around. You have to work as if you were starting from scratch. There's really no safety in playing it safe.

Take the "Mirror" Test

Before trying to turn a church around, there are several questions you must ask that will help you look critically at the church. Your answers will help you decide if the time is right.

- Is your church flexible enough to face the future?
- Is change necessary?
- How urgent is the need for change?
- Will your people need lengthy preparation before changes can be made?

- Do you have the money or other resources to institute change?
- What barriers to change exist?
- Is there trust between leaders and the congregation?
- What changes must be made?

Preparing for Change

If your answers to the preceding questions seem to indicate that the time is right for change, you will need to do the following.

Control any damage. If you have made mistakes, own up to them immediately and correct them even faster. Establish high morals, ethics, and credibility, and stick to your standards. Show your people daily that these principles are more than words—they live and thrive in you. Leaders who lack such principles are doomed to fail.

Create a focus for change. Recruit a small group of the most committed and forward-thinking people to spearhead the effort. Give them special training and a variety of experiences to make them experts in change management.

Define your church's purpose, vision, and values. Use strategy meetings or retreats to formulate purpose, vision, and core values statements. Refine these statements until they can stand as significant, meaningful, believable, and actionable guides for everyone in your church.

Listen to the unchurched. Pay more attention to what people outside your church want. What are they saying? Why don't they come to your church? What would draw them to you?

Lift morale. When times are bad, the morale of the people may fall to a low point. Lift their morale by asking for their input and sharing your plans for change. Keep people abreast of results. Start prayer groups that focus on asking

God for future direction. Morale will improve as people see results from their prayers and actions.

Communicate well to your people. Visit every ministry on a regular time schedule. Communicate to your people a minimum of twelve times a year concerning your purpose, vision, and the overall progress of your church toward its goals. Be candid with everyone.

Make the hard decisions. Face reality as it is, not as it was or as you wish it were. You can't turn a church around with half measures. Be sure to go far enough! Half measures will give you less than halfway results! The key word is *proactive.* Control your destiny, or something else will.

Focus on your core ministries. To accomplish more, try doing less. Narrow your focus and reduce your programs (those not honestly needed). With key leaders, make a list on a chalkboard of all the ministries and programs your church conducts. Underline the ones that are absolutely needed. What *must* your church continue to do? If possible, eliminate the rest.

To identify your core ministries, look at all your church ministries and categorize them in the following groups.

Stars: The most profitable ministries—the ones that are responsible for bringing in the most new people or reaching the most people for Christ.

Puzzles: The ministries that appear to be good but aren't producing the results you think they should.

Plow horses: The popular ministries that don't honestly result in many newer people coming to Christ or your church but you must keep.

Dogs: The ministries that are draining your church of resources and produce almost no results. Deal with dogs by retooling them, reinventing them, or replacing them with stars.

Start a new ministry. The underlying factor for success is the willingness to fall down, pick yourself up, and start over again. The rules for starting new ministries are: Do it, try it, fix it. Start a minimum of one new ministry each year.

Use action teams. Assign each team to accomplish a single goal and celebrate when it is reached. Teams allow people to buy into new concepts from the beginning and share their diversity of experience. In short, they build ownership.

Remember, your church will not be fixed in a year. Generally it takes five to seven years to turn a city church around and ten to twelve years to turn a rural church around.

20

COMING BACK
AFTER DISASTER

How do you bring your church back from disaster? How do you help your people pick themselves up off the floor, put the past behind them, and confidently face the future?

Disaster may threaten your church following accidental parenthood (a church split), a physical disaster (sanctuary burns down), a moral dilemma (pastoral impropriety), or a number of other events. Turning a church around from one of these or other potential disasters takes patience, creativity, and a sound strategy.

Enemies All Around

Churches that experience a disaster have at least five common enemies they must face and conquer. These enemies are:

Low morale. People who have spent years or even months in a pressure cooker atmosphere will be discouraged. They may even be angry that God has let this happen to them. Lost dreams, threatened security, and feeling all beat up will result in low morale.

Survival mode. People will take a defensive position to protect themselves from further hurt and danger. This means they will resist new ways of doing things and creative solutions to problems. Wanting only to protect what is left, they function in a survival mode.

Passive attitudes. People will cling to a wait-and-see attitude, hedging their bets. Attempts to recruit new people into all church ministry areas will meet with a so-so response because of their passive attitudes. Many will view ministry as a trap and refuse to get involved.

Consolidated power. Leaders will grab the power and keep decision making close to home, trying to consolidate their control over all church functions. Anyone seeking to challenge their newfound control will be met with strong resistance. Anything perceived as threatening the calm will be fiercely challenged.

Loss of respect. If the pastor is perceived to have caused the crisis, directly or indirectly, his ministry will be viewed with skepticism, and often people will lose respect for the pastoral office. A new pastor will face resistance due to this loss of respect for months or years to come.

Ten Steps for Turning a Church Around

There are ten steps that leaders must take to turn a church around. And remember this principle: Turnaround must come from the bottom up, not from the top down. Thus, while church leaders must take action, the congregation must be committed to change and participate in it for the turnaround to occur.

1. *Get close to the people.* Get to know people. Listen to them. Hear their concerns. People need reassurance that others are there for them.

2. *Take control of the cash.* Immediately determine the fixed amount of cash the church needs each month. Fixed expenses include utilities, rent or mortgage, and salaries—essentially the necessities to keep running. While leaders may not want direct control of the cash, they should participate in the decisions for spending money. To stay solvent, spend only what was brought in last month. Then you will always be solvent for thirty days.

3. *Find the positives.* Even though the positives may be difficult to spot, every situation has them. For example, once people get over the shock of their church building burning down, they begin to see the positives of rebuilding a newer structure that will be better suited for ministry today.

4. *Create a new vision for the future.* Only a new vision will enable people to pick themselves up off the floor, put the past behind them, and face the future. Put together a vision sermon that you can believe yourself. Share your vision as often as you can wherever you can.

5. *Stress your mission and purpose.* Print your mission statement on a little plastic card that each person can carry in his or her pocket, billfold, or purse.

6. *Give people a way to feel good about themselves.* Pat them on the back for the way they've handled the pressure.

7. *Design situations in which your people can succeed.* Look for short-term projects or goals that you know your people can reach. Lead them to work toward those goals. When they have reached them, celebrate the victory. Gradually people will be able to adopt larger goals or projects.

8. *Use the best you have.* A wise pastor once said, "You've got to use what you've got." Begin using the best leaders, musicians, and teachers you currently have in your church. As you faithfully serve God with your present resources, God will bring you additional ones as they are needed.

9. *Communicate, communicate, communicate.* Give people specifics. Explain exactly how each person, class, or group

can contribute to the turnaround. Keep people informed through letters sent to them at home.

10. *Devise a plan.* As you talk to people, survey the situation, and articulate the positives, a plan will begin to form. List your options under these headings:

- What we must do immediately.
- What should be done in six months or next year.
- What can wait more than a year.

21

RELOCATING A CHURCH

It used to be common practice to plant churches in quiet neighborhoods well away from the major flow of traffic. Today's approach is to place churches as close to the traffic flow as possible. Busy streets are better than quiet lanes for attracting guests.

This change in philosophy is causing some older churches to consider relocating for the purpose of renewed ministry and growth.

Ten Steps for Relocating

Churches that have relocated suggest the following general steps for thinking through the relocation process.

1. *Seek the Lord in prayer.* It is best not to relocate just to relocate. God must be directing your move based on his eternal purposes.
2. *Involve key leaders.* Include all formal leaders as well as informal leaders in the relocation process.

3. *Interview other church leaders.* Contact the leaders of other churches that have relocated to get their recommendations. What worked? What would they do differently?

4. *Conduct a feasibility study.* What are the advantages and disadvantages of a move? Do the study yourself or, better yet, hire a consulting firm to do it for you.

5. *Conduct a demographic study.* Where is the best new location for your church? In what location would your church most likely be able to prosper and grow?

6. *Develop a relocation plan.* Establish short- and long-range goals as a timetable for relocating. Communicate these goals, being certain to update everyone on a regular basis.

7. *Be available to your people.* Be very sensitive to all your people. Make personal appointments with those who need to talk with you about the future changes. Love and nurture them throughout the transition by listening to their hurts and concerns.

8. *Locate a temporary place to hold services during the transition.* You most likely will need a temporary location for one to five years, particularly if you need to sell the previous building. Seek to find an interim meeting place as close as possible to your eventual permanent location.

9. *Plan and organize well.* Most disappointments in the relocation process come through poor planning. Take nothing for granted. Plan each step. Use the services of a consultant.

10. *Make your move.* Move as soon as possible. The longer the wait the greater the chance for discouragement.

Dos and Don'ts

Churches that have successfully gone through the relocation process suggest the following *dos* and *don'ts* as keys to a successful move.

DO develop a renewed vision to reach people for Christ. The main purpose for relocating a church must be directly tied to Christ's command to "make disciples of all the nations." Relocate because you have a vision to reach people.

DON'T relocate simply because of problems or difficulties. Seek to resolve any internal problems before you move. If you don't, many of them will simply move with you.

DO package the vision for relocation in terms of carrying on the past vision of the church. Focus on how the new location will help continue the vision of the founders of your church. Express the new vision in terms of the old vision to win people to Christ.

DON'T move until church leaders are convinced it is essential to move. Pastors and leaders must believe solidly in relocation. A minimum of 80 percent, and hopefully 90 percent, of the church must be for the relocation. People must believe it is God's will.

DO organize a relocation task force to coordinate the move. It will take a team effort to relocate a church successfully. If the leadership for such a move rests only on the pastor's shoulders, or on a few board members, the potential for success is severely reduced. A special task force is needed, because the regular boards and committees will be too busy holding things together during the move.

DON'T begin many new programs during the relocation process. Even in the best situations, new programs or ministries take a huge amount of energy. During a relocation process, much energy will be expended on the transition, leaving little for beginning new programs.

DO develop a support system to relieve stress on the senior pastor. It is not unusual for a senior pastor to leave shortly after a church relocation. The stress of the relocation process on the pastor and the potential for burnout are high. If a church hopes to keep their pastor following a major move, they must pray for him during the entire transition process and give him extra time off to relax.

DON'T be afraid to incur reasonable debt. Once a decision is made to move, the longer the church waits before moving, the more momentum will be lost. While going into unnecessary debt is unwise, delaying a move too long for lack of funding is also unwise.

DO relocate as quickly as possible. The average church going through a relocation process moves within twelve months of the final decision to relocate. This move may be to a temporary location while the new building is under construction.

- 40 percent move in less than six months.
- 30 percent take more than one year.
- 30 percent move within six to twelve months.

DON'T be afraid to get outside help. A consultant can help a church establish new vision and set clear plans for relocating to a more effective area. While church leaders may be able to do the planning, an outside consultant is a source of unbiased information that will help a church avoid potential difficulties.

DO establish a presence in the new community before you get there. Use small groups, advertising, seminars, and workshops to let the new community know who you are. Saturate the new area with direct mail, alerting the people to your coming.

DON'T take lightly the fears of your people. In most cases, 10 percent of the people in a church will be unable to relocate to the new church site. Develop a plan to help them find a new church. Visit people in their homes to hear and answer questions they may have concerning the move to a new location.

DO get people to the new site for a visit. Usually there is a period of time between locating a new site and moving to it. While a building is under construction or a facility is being remodeled, take church members to the new location to see the progress that is being made.

DON'T relocate without a thorough demographic study. Complete a demographic study of several potential new areas to determine the best place to move. Find out what groups of people reside in the potential areas and determine the ones your church would be best suited to reach with the gospel.

DO develop a strategy on how to reach people in the new ministry area. Write out a characterization of the unchurched people in your new ministry area and then detail several strategic plans to reach them with the Good News of Christ. Think through how to attract them to your church and how to assimilate them once they come.

DON'T neglect to study church planting strategies. Do your homework by reading books and attending seminars on church planting. You will find research on church planting strategies relevant to your relocation process.

Experienced real estate salespeople know the top three concerns for a good home are location, location, and location. Perhaps the same could be said about a good church home.

PART 8

PASTORAL COMPENSATION

22

NEGOTIATING SALARY

When I first began pastoring, my mind was on things like preaching, visitation, and counseling. Little did I realize that I needed to understand how to negotiate my salary.

Like most pastors, if there was one thing I didn't want to talk about, it was money, especially when it related directly to my salary. I especially wanted to avoid the appearance of greed.

In 1 Peter 5:2 pastors are told to "shepherd the flock of God among you, exercising oversight not under compulsion, but voluntarily, according to the will of God; and not for sordid gain, but with eagerness." Another translation of this passage calls money "filthy lucre" and I wanted to stay away from "filthy lucre."

I found that, if I talked about money too much, it drove a wedge between others in the church and me. It became obvious to me that, if I was to be able to minister effectively to people, I couldn't talk about my salary.

I guess I just expected God's people to take care of me in a fair and equitable manner. However, I began to learn that, while God's people often have good intentions when it comes to providing for their pastors, they don't always follow through very well.

Now I don't think pastors should begin to organize a pastors' union to present their case to the Christian community. But I do believe pastors need to take more of a proactive position in negotiating their salary.

Practical Guidelines

These guidelines certainly aren't the final word on how to handle salary negotiations, but they may give you some ideas you can begin to use right where you are serving.

Negotiate a Good Starting Salary

When accepting a new ministry position, seek as high a salary as possible. It's easier to negotiate an entry-level salary than a salary increase once inside an organization. This is true for a number of reasons. For one, when churches are looking to fill a vacant position, they usually have done their homework and know what others are being paid in similar staff positions.

Tied directly to this, of course, is the natural desire of the church to win the person they really want. When a church is interested in a particular candidate, they often will offer a higher salary with additional benefits to convince the person to accept the position.

Since most churches give more thought to the importance of compensation when looking for a pastor than when trying to keep him, it's wise for a pastoral candidate to negotiate as high a compensation package as possible when first taking a position.

Use Your Network

Occasionally I've found a high level of frustration, anger, and even bitterness among pastors and their spouses over the issue of compensation. One pastor I know handled his anger by writing the names of frustrating board members on his golf balls. Later, while at the driving range, he released his emotions by soundly striking each ball.

Obviously that's not a good way to handle anger. The physical exercise may have relieved some stress, but it didn't get him the desired raise. Here are some better ideas:

- Tell your frustrations to the Lord in prayer.
- Share your feelings with some of your loyal supporters.
- Talk to those who have the power to make the final decision on the compensation package.
- Arrange a meeting with decision makers over breakfast or lunch when you can honestly share your frustrations.
- Write a short letter to the appropriate board members, noting some needs and frustrations you have in the area of compensation.

Devise a Review System

Most churches promise a salary review but few actually do it. If you hope to create an atmosphere in which you may freely negotiate your compensation package, you'll need to develop a workable review system. Here are some ideas:

- Schedule a salary review early in the budgeting process.
- Schedule an interview in which you and your spouse can discuss your needs with the appropriate people.
- Determine an initial proposal.
- Take a week to pray and think over the proposal before it is finalized.
- Give leaders honest comments.
- Accept their decision.

Compare Apples with Apples

Often church leaders will look at a pastor's total compensation package and compare it to their own cash salaries. They then figure that the pastor is making much more than he actually is, since, compared to their take-home pay, the pastor's total pay seems high.

The difficulty lies in comparing apples with oranges, rather than apples with apples. For example, when you ask the average layperson how much he or she makes, the person will usually give you the take-home pay. They will almost never include the hidden costs of employer contributions to social security, retirement, or medical insurance. These hidden costs will often add as much as 40 percent to an individual's cash salary.

Yet when the same layperson looks at the pastor's salary, he or she includes all of the benefits in the salary package, rather than just the cash salary.

Here are some ideas on how the church should view the pastor's salary:

- Separate cash salary from benefits and reimbursements in the church budget.
- Consider reimbursements a cost of doing business.

Set Salary Standards

It is good to have some objective standards by which salaries will be set. Since church board members change from year to year, this is especially critical. Even though you arrive at a workable formula with one board, you may find next year's board has a different viewpoint. Salary standards will help stabilize changes due to fluctuations in board personnel from year to year.

Here are some ideas for the board to consider:

- Determine what percentage of the total church budget will go for salaries.

- Develop a procedure for determining a base cash salary.
- Set an amount as a yearly supplement for experience.
- Determine what major benefits will be offered and how they will be increased.
- Figure the normal costs of doing business and a procedure for reimbursement.

Trusting God

It still holds true that we are to "seek first His kingdom and His righteousness, and all these things will be added to you" (Matt. 6:33). This, of course, holds true for very practical matters, like increases in our compensation. We need to trust in God's supply.

But I believe it's appropriate for pastors to speak honestly to their church leaders about their material needs. So take the initiative and use some of these ideas to negotiate your compensation package this coming year. I think you'll be glad you did.

23

DEVELOPING
A COMPENSATION PLAN

Most church boards honestly want to be fair with their pastors when it comes to salary. The following are some ideas on how to develop a pay plan that is equitable. As the board seeks to develop a pastoral compensation plan, it should keep in mind these guidelines.

- The priority for expenditure of money should be in the order of staff, ministry, and buildings.
- In small churches the pastor's salary package will normally be 50 to 60 percent of the total church budget.
- In large churches the total salaries and benefit packages for all staff will normally be 40 to 50 percent of the total budget.

There are four main methods that churches use to determine pastoral salaries:

The flat-rate method. Using this method a church board assigns an arbitrary salary to a pastor with little regard to experience, training, and other critical factors. It is a simple method to use but usually results in irregular salary evaluation, often allowing a pastor to go years without much of an increase.

The experience and role method. This method is built on the assumption that those with the most years of experience and the greatest responsibility deserve the highest compensation. It is better than the flat-rate method but may lead to inequity among staff doing similar work.

The comparable worth method. This method is developed by comparing pastoral staff positions with secular jobs requiring similar training, experience, and responsibility. Many churches use the salary guidelines for public school teachers and administrators to determine staff salaries.

The base salary method. Using this method the board establishes a base salary for the senior staff position and then other staff positions are calculated as an index of that standard. Supplements are added for experience, education, and other factors.

A Suggested Model

The base salary model is an equitable way to develop a compensation plan. It has several advantages over the other models:

- *It provides guidelines for advancement.* A new staff person may be brought in at one level and then, after gaining experience, advance to the next level.
- *It provides incentive for effective ministry.* The clear steps of promotion will give pastoral staff an added incentive for fulfilling their roles. As a pastor's ministry grows, so will his or her position and salary.
- *It provides objectivity for salary negotiation.* With this method, real or imagined inequities between people doing similar work are eliminated.

As an example, let's assume a senior pastor's annual base salary is $50,000. With this base, an equitable salary index for all other paid staff in a local church might be as follows:

Position	Salary	Index
Senior Pastor	$50,000	1.00
Associate Pastor	$42,500	.85
Assistant Pastor	$37,500	.75
Youth Pastor	$32,500	.65
Director	$27,500	.55
Secretary	$22,500	.45
Custodian	$17,500	.35
Clerical Worker	$12,500	.25

Note: Base salaries are figured on a twelve-month year. Those who work part-time receive a percentage of the applicable base according to the actual time worked. Supplements for experience, education, and other benefits are additional.

Establishing an Equitable Base

The foundation of this model is the establishment of an equitable base salary. One way to do this in any area of the United States is to key the base salary to the cost of purchasing a home in that geographical area.

According to conventional mortgage underwriting guidelines, the maximum amount of income that can be allocated to mortgage payments is 28 percent. Using these figures as a guide, an average base salary should be approximately 3.5 times the monthly mortgage. For example, if it costs $1,000 per month to own a home, the base salary would be $3,500 per month or $42,000 per year (3.5 x 1,000 x 12).

Establishing an equitable base pay may not be as easy as this appears. There are other variables to consider:

- Churches that are unable to provide a base salary that allows a pastor to purchase an average home might consider providing interest-free or shared equity loans that will reduce the pastor's monthly payment for the home to one-third or less of his cash salary.

- Small churches that are unable to provide a base salary keyed to housing costs may be able to key the base salary to rental housing costs.
- Pastoral staff who have come to a church at various times may have differing housing costs. Newer staff may actually have greater needs than senior staff who were able to purchase a home at an earlier time.
- Pastoral staff who are at various stages of life will have varying needs.

In general a base salary must be equitable when compared to:

The salaries of people of equal education and experience in the same church. Pastors realize they will likely never receive salaries equal to those working in secular jobs. However, laypeople must not expect their pastors to live in homes and on salaries that are considerably below the standards the laypeople would accept.

The salaries of other staff in the same church. In multiple staff situations, salaries must be balanced between positions. Gaps greater than 15 percent between neighboring positions on the staff chain may result in hurt feelings that will undermine staff relationships and effective ministry.

Although it is difficult to prove a direct cause and effect relationship, most church growth consultants are in agreement that the length of a pastor's tenure has a direct influence on the growth potential of a church. Providing an equitable cash salary is one positive way to ensure pastoral longevity and increase your growth potential.

24

SUPPLEMENTS, BENEFITS, AND REIMBURSEMENTS

Important additions to the base salary model in the last chapter are salary supplements, benefits, and reimbursements. *Supplements* affect directly the cash salary received by pastoral staff. They include compensation for experience, education, and ordination. *Benefits* are additions above the cash salary. They include items like paid vacation, health insurance, and contributions to a retirement fund. *Reimbursements* are direct payments for expenses incurred in conducting normal work for such things as travel, meals, and lodging.

Salary Supplements

Salary supplements are added to the base salary of each individual according to a fixed guideline. The following is a suggested schedule.

Experience

Years	Supplement
1	1%
2	2%
3	3%
4	4%
5	5%
6	7%
7	9%
8	11%
9	13%
10	15%

For example, a senior pastor with six years experience and a base of $50,000 would receive a supplement of 7 percent or $3,500 for his years of experience. Note: This system rewards the staff person who establishes a longer tenure.

Education

Degree	Supplement
Master's	3%
Special (counseling, etc.)	6%
Doctorate	9%

For example, a senior pastor with six years experience and a master's degree and a license in marital counseling would receive $56,500. This is a base of $50,000 plus $3,500 for tenure and $3,000 (6 percent) for his master's degree and advanced degree in marital counseling. Note: Only the highest percentage for education is used. They are not added together.

There are other variables that should have an effect on the salaries of pastoral staff.

Ordination: The base salary is set with the assumption that the pastoral positions are staffed with ordained individuals. If this is not the case, it is recommended that $1,000 be deducted from the base salary for a person not licensed or ordained. Then add $500 when the person is licensed and another $500 when he is ordained. Positions not normally calling for ordained individuals, such as a custodian, are not affected.

Continuing education: As in other professions, continuing education is a must for today's pastors. It is recommended that 1 percent of a person's base salary be added for books, subscriptions, and newsletters and 2 percent of the base salary be added for the cost of seminars and continuing education courses at various schools. For example, a pastor with a base salary of $30,000 would receive an additional $300 for books and $600 for seminars. Note: These expenses could be handled as reimbursements rather than part of the salary.

Social Security: Self-employed pastors pay a higher individual rate for Social Security than they would if they were considered employees of the church. It is recommended that the church either supplement their pastors' base salaries to make up the difference or begin paying employee withholding for them. The church should consult with a tax expert for advice.

Benefits

Often churches would like to offer a complete benefits package to their staff, but just meeting the budget may leave the cupboards bare. While it is not good to give extra perks if this would jeopardize a church's financial stability, such extras should be given when possible, for they will attract and keep quality people.

Fringe benefits are good for the staff person and church alike. Many fringe benefits are not subject to tax and thus they provide compensation that exceeds the dollar amount spent by the church. The most obvious example for pastors is a housing allowance, which is not subject to income tax (although it is subject to Social Security tax).

A church board must decide which fringe benefits to give to which employees. Benefits that they should consider for all the staff are:

- paid sick leave
- paid holidays
- paid vacation
- paid sabbatical leave every five to seven years
- paid personal days
- paid professional days
- paid time off for military training
- paid time off for jury duty
- tuition for advanced education
- insurance (life, health, cancer, disability, professional liability, workmen's compensation, dental, vision)
- trips to professional meetings (accompanied by spouse once a year)
- retirement (minimum $2,000 per year)
- loan for home purchase (or shared equity or other assistance)
- tuition assistance for children

Reimbursements

Recent changes in the tax law have made it advantageous for churches to simply reimburse pastors for expenses rather than including estimated amounts as a portion of cash salaries. Church leaders should establish a budget line amount that would be reimbursed to pastors with supporting receipts. For example, reimbursements should be made for travel, meals, lodging, gifts, benevolent gifts, professional books, subscriptions, continuing education, and expenses incurred at church meetings and conventions.

Additional Recommendations

It is recommended that full-time pastoral staff receive a minimum of four weeks paid vacation. Church boards should take into consideration that pastors are on call at all hours of the day or night, which can cause stress and burnout—a major reason pastors leave a church. If churches were more sensitive to their pastors' need for several weeks of paid vacation, pastoral tenure could be increased.

It is recommended that full-time pastoral staff receive two weeks paid study leave (continuing education) per year. Church boards should take the initiative to make certain their pastoral staff keep up to date in their field of expertise. This is especially important for teaching and preaching pastors.

It is recommended that pastoral staff receive retirement benefits. Although it does not happen as often today as it did in the past, many pastors still reach retirement with little or nothing to live on. Church boards should take responsibility for seeing that their pastors are financially prepared for retirement.

Developing an equitable pastoral compensation plan is difficult, but when a church takes the time to do it, they find it increases staff morale, ensures pastoral longevity, and promotes healthier ministry. And, perhaps more important, God is pleased that the church has taken care of his appointed servants (see Eph. 4:11–12).

PART 9

DEVELOPING
MINISTRY

25

CHILDREN'S MINISTRY

Ministry to children has changed since many of us were in elementary school. A popular comparison notes that fifty years ago, the top seven problems in public schools were talking, chewing gum, making noise, running in the halls, getting out of line, wearing improper clothes, and not putting paper in the wastebasket.

Now the top seven problems in public schools are drug abuse, alcohol abuse, pregnancy, suicide, rape, robbery, and assault.

Changing Ministry

Effective ministry to today's children goes beyond a basic understanding of development issues or simple babysitting. It requires taking risks to walk alongside children weighed down with burdens of divorce; physical, emotional, and sexual abuse; overly committed parents; and stress-related disorders.

Children in the fourth, fifth, and sixth grades often demonstrate a strange mixture of sophistication and childlike qualities. These "little adults" are more like the junior highers of twenty years ago than the elementary students most of us recall. Exposure to adult pressures has resulted in children who might be characterized best as "elementary teenagers."

Reaching Children

As you seek to develop your children's ministry to reach the new generation coming into your church, consider doing the following.

Survey other churches. When visiting other churches, notice how they advertise their children's ministry to the church body. Review the curriculum they have chosen and ask why they have found the curriculum to be effective. Tour the classrooms, nursery, and offices, jotting down ideas.

Train children's workers. Try the "fifth Sunday training" approach. Four times a year there will be five Sundays in a month. On this fifth Sunday schedule for current children's workers a one-hour or one-and-a-half-hour event to include testimonies of significant accomplishments in the children's ministry, a time for prayer, and skill development training in some area of children's ministry.

Target preadolescents. Since the times are changing and fifth and sixth grade children are becoming more sophisticated, this age group is fast becoming the black hole of dropouts in the church. Most churches have not kept up with the times and have not incorporated new ideas for reaching the preadolescent. Select a new curriculum aimed at preadolescents and begin a ministry targeted to them this year.

Hire a children's pastor. Children's ministry is often one of the most overlooked areas of ministry. Hiring a children's pastor, even if it begins as a part-time position, will signal a new commitment to caring for children. A children's pastor is a vital ingredient of a holistic ministry to the entire family.

Establish a prayer base. There is a tremendous amount of pressure on children and their families today. Our families certainly need a prayer covering. The children's workers who are trying to reach these families also need to be held up in prayer. Begin by establishing a small prayer group to consistently pray for your children and workers.

Highlight the children's ministry. Have the pastor interview children in front of the congregation. Give monthly updates in the services to help the congregation know how they should be praying for the children's ministry. Create a yearly video presentation highlighting some of the major accomplishments that have taken place during the year. Show how lives have changed due to the focus and energy of this ministry. Provide a quality brochure that describes the children's ministry for all newcomers to the church.

Build ownership of the children's ministry throughout the church. One of the best ways to help the congregation take ownership of the children's ministry is to have adults pray for each child. On 3" x 5" cards put down relevant information about every child connected to your ministry. Then give the cards to people from the congregation who will be willing for a month (or quarter) to pray each week for the child. Such a ministry helps build bridges between the generations and automatically increases adult interest in and support of the children's ministry. Also it may increase your base of volunteers and/or workers as adults develop more of a burden for the children of your church.

26

THE BEST CHILD CARE

Excellent child care has always been an important part of growing churches. Parents are naturally concerned for their children and want them capably cared for while the adults participate in church activities.

Our changing lifestyle has meant that child care has become a major component of our society. While parents throughout history have loved and cared for their children, today's parents approach child care differently than those of only twenty years ago.

Today's Parents

Today's parents are starting a new baby boom. More than four million babies were born in 2001 in the United States. That year marked fifteen straight years of 3.8 million or more births per year in the United States. This higher birth-rate trend shows no sign of abating.

Insight: Parents will be bringing a new wave of young children into your church nursery.

Today's parents are older than those of past years. Approximately one-sixth of all first-time parents are over the age of thirty. They get out of school with master's degrees at twenty-five to thirty, and that's when they begin to have children.

Insight: Older parents expect more of your nursery than do younger parents.

Today's parents are spending more money on their children. Americans have increased their spending for infant and toddler clothing by 120 percent over the last decade. It is not unusual for today's parents to spend more than a thousand dollars decorating a baby's room and more than three hundred dollars to furnish it with toys.

Insight: Parents expect your church's nursery to be as well equipped as their baby's room at home.

Today's parents want the best for their children. Since many of today's couples in their thirties are just beginning to have children, many families are small, with only one or two children. Parents tend to provide these children with the best of everything. Nike, Chanel, Ralph Lauren, Guess, and Christian Dior are among the many big-name designers who now make infant or toddler clothes.

Insight: Parents expect your church to provide the best for their children.

Today's parents have less time for their children. Parents are having kids when their careers are taking off, so they have less time at home than did earlier generations of parents. They have more money and shower their children with material things as a way to show their love.

Insight: Parents expect your church to express the same love for their children that they do.

Today's parents are experienced child care shoppers. Today many parents hire other people to take care of their children during the workday. Whether they choose to place their children in day care centers or with in-home care providers, they are experienced at shopping for quality care.

Insight: Parents expect your nursery to provide the same quality care they would find at the best day care centers.

Checklist

Since growing churches are ministering to more and more young families, your child care program and facility are of vital importance to your entire ministry. Use the following checklist as an idea starter to create an attractive nursery.

Redecorate your nursery every other year to keep it up to date. As times change, so must the carpet, designs, colors, furniture, and accessories in your nursery. Cute animals are always in style. One year it may be dinosaurs, another year ducks. Today you see cows all over the place.

Sanitize your nursery weekly. Parents notice whether your nursery is clean or dirty. Regularly sanitize all surfaces, toys, tables, trays, bedding, and bibs. Place used toys in a bin marked for washing and clean them each week. Clean carpets every other month. Clean walls every month.

Evaluate the ratio of children to nursery workers. With trained child care professionals, there should be no more than four infants per worker and no more than five toddlers per worker. If you use volunteer workers, it is best if there are no more than two infants or four toddlers per worker.

Provide a hazard-free nursery. Replace broken toys, torn books, and damaged furniture. Fix peeling paint, protruding nails, leaky plumbing, and lighting problems. Separate toddlers from babies, since toddlers could unknowingly hurt an infant. Check fire alarms on a regular basis. Maintain good ventilation, heating, and air-conditioning.

Develop a nursery policy. Your nursery policy should contain information on how discipline is handled, procedures in case of sickness or accident, age guidelines, hours of operation, wellness policies, use of volunteers, registration procedures, and a fire escape plan. Provide a copy to all parents and post one near the nursery entrance.

Use the same nursery care workers. When parents see the same people working in the nursery week after week, they begin to trust them to give their children the best care. A high turnover rate of nursery workers keeps children and parents from building relationships. Rotate workers as little as possible.

Train all nursery workers. Tell them what you want and how their ministry fits into the overall philosophy of your church. Require workers to take first aid training and CPR for infants and children. Hire nursery workers who interact well with children.

27

FIFTIES-PLUS MINISTRY

One of the facts that church leaders are in agreement on is that the number of people in the church who are over fifty is increasing at a significant rate never before seen. For example, consider the following perspective of a congregation of five hundred members throughout the years, with a prediction into the year 2030.

Year	Church of 500
1900	21 members were 65 or older
1976	54 members were 65 or older
1986	125 members were 65 or older
1996	168 members were 65 or older
2030	230—about half—will be over 65!

It is estimated that by 2020 churches will experience a 74 percent increase in people over fifty years old, while seeing only a 1 percent increase in people under fifty. This rapid aging of our congregations is being driven by the large Baby Boomer population, who are now in their forties and fifties. In 1996 a Boomer turned fifty years old every 8.4 seconds. In

2001 a Boomer turned fifty every 6.8 seconds. Or another way to look at it is that about eleven thousand Boomers will turn fifty each day for another ten years! It is therefore no surprise that churches throughout the United States are responding with fifties-plus ministries. However, most are making a big mistake.

The Big Mistake

The biggest mistake churches are making is the assumption that aging Boomers will be like aging Builders—the generation preceding them. Like the commercial says: "This isn't your father's Oldsmobile." Aging Boomers are not your typical Builders. By their sheer numbers, Boomers have always redefined whatever they have come in contact with, and middle age is nothing different! For example, in 1900 we defined the following six life stages:

birth
childhood (1–12 years)
adolescence (13–18 years)
adulthood (19–65 years)
old age (66+ years)
death

Today, due to longer life spans and changing maturation rates of our children, Boomers are identifying eleven life stages as follows:

birth
early childhood (0–4 years)
childhood (5–10 years)
preadolescence (11–12 years)
adolescence (13–17 years)
emerging adults (18–30 years)

young adults (31–50 years)
middle adults (51–70 years)
senior adults (71–80 years)
elderly adults (81+ years)
death

The New Fifties-Plus Ministry

It is not easy to design a fifties-plus ministry for today's Boomers. Most of them demand a different array of services than did the same age group a generation ago. The best advice is to scrap all conventional wisdom about ministry to older persons and start from scratch. Here are ten key ministry insights to keep in mind:

Middle-aged Boomers will be different from middle-aged Builders. Personality does not change much after thirty years of age. Fifties-plus Boomers will not suddenly wake up and like older forms of ministry. Expect middle-aged Boomers to continue to ask, "Why?" and to expect you to "Tell it like it is" and "Let it all hang out." They will continue to prefer informal and unstructured activities, expect change and variety, think the system is the problem, be cause-oriented, desire to experience life, and have a low view of institutions.

In short: Expect fifties-plus Boomers to act and think in much the same way they always have but with more maturity.

Middle-aged Boomers will continue to be offended by stereotypes. They do not want to be seen as frail, old, or sedentary. They like to be considered active, alert, contributors, experienced, healthy, independent, and hard working, and they usually are. Most Boomers entering their fifties think of themselves as about thirty-five years old.

In short: When structuring fifties-plus ministry, keep in mind that Boomers want to be active and giving not just receiving.

Middle-aged Boomers will continue to aspire to be young!
They have never desired to wear any fashion that made
them look mature, and the whole notion of staying young
forever is very strong.

In short: Any fifties-plus program that looks like it was designed
for their parents will not attract Boomers. To be successful a
fifties-plus ministry must appear youthful!

*Middle-aged Boomers will continue to see themselves as unique
individuals.* They have always directed their own lives
and resist the "poor dear syndrome." They dislike senior
discounts because they reflect a stereotyped ageism. In
their way of thinking, a 10 percent discount means they
are 10 percent depreciated.

In short: Fifties-plus Boomers are interested only in a ministry
that is healthy, vibrant, and worthy of their time and energy.
Since they are not apt to respond to a ministry developed for
them, make them part of the planning team for any fifties-plus
ministry you start.

*Middle-aged Boomers will continue to search for the next ad-
venture and look for new experiences.* Note the popularity
of sports utility vehicles: Fifties-plus Boomers never drive
them off road, but they have an adventure from their
driveway to the grocery store and back!

In short: Expect fifties-plus Boomers to be attracted to a ministry
that provides adventure and new experiences.

Middle-aged Boomers will continue to spend money. The *New
York Times* reports that empty-nest Boomers are creating
a new phenomenon. Instead of buying a smaller home
when their kids move out, they buy a bigger one.

In short: Expect your fifties-plus attendees to be attracted to
and support ministries that are high quality and will make a
difference in their lives.

Middle-aged Boomers will continue to accelerate their careers.
As they enter their fifties and sixties, they will change their

lifestyle, but they will stay involved in the workforce. Note the recent decision by Congress to eliminate the work penalty of those between sixty-five and seventy years old.

In short: Expect fifties-plus Boomers to be attracted to ministries that allow for their work schedules.

Middle-aged Boomers will continue to look back and leap forward. Notice the successful return of the VW bug, Glen Campbell concerts, A&E's *Biography*, and public television's recent Paul Anka concert.

In short: Expect fifties-plus Boomers to be attracted to a ministry that helps them look back, while at the same time launching another chapter in their lives.

Middle-aged Boomers will continue to search for balance. With the importance of family never having been so high, fifties-plus Boomers are enjoying the balance that grandchildren bring to life.

In short: Expect fifties-plus Boomers to struggle with the same spiritual and emotional issues that all generations have struggled with.

Middle-aged Boomers will continue to break the rules. They have always challenged the rules and will continue to do so while reinventing themselves.

In short: Offer middle-aged Boomers a ministry that gives them a chance to break the rules. In other words, pique their curiosity and encourage them to try new approaches.

Three Alternatives

Churches have three alternatives as they seek to minister to fifties-plus Boomers. The *first alternative* is to do nothing special to plan, program, attract, or serve the emerging fifties-plus generation. Observation confirms this is the option that churches choose most often.

The *second alternative* is to develop a ministry of care for middle-aged people, including classes, fellowship groups, and pot lucks. Observation confirms this is not likely to attract middle-aged Boomers.

The *third alternative* is to develop a challenging ministry whereby middle-aged Boomers become actively involved in serving and giving to others. Observation confirms this is the most effective alternative. Which alternative is your church using?

PART 10

SMALL GROUPS

28

SMALL-GROUP MINISTRY

The Christian life is not a solo journey. For Joshua to be victorious, he needed the support of Moses, Aaron, and Hur (Exod. 17:8–15). For us to be victorious in our Christian lives, we need the support of brothers and sisters in Jesus Christ.

In our fast-paced society, people are often finding their support through a variety of small-group experiences. A small group is a group of three to twelve people who meet face-to-face on a regular time schedule and have a sense of accountability to each other and to Jesus Christ. The key elements are:

- *Three to twelve people.* The group is small enough for face-to-face relationships to take place.
- *Face-to-face.* People interface with each other directly and personally.
- *Regular time schedule.* The group meets a minimum of two times per month.
- *Sense of accountability.* The group has a feeling of concern and responsibility to each other.

Why Small Groups?

The following are ten reasons why you should consider a small-group ministry in your church.

Developing relationships. If people are to function as God intended, there must be an intentional effort to improve interpersonal relationships. This is best accomplished as people gather together in small groups for personal care and support.

The power of working together. The combined strength of two is greater than two times the strength of one. Two working together can accomplish more than two working alone. "Two are better than one because they have a good reward for their labor" (Eccles. 4:9).

Jesus' model. Jesus modeled the necessity for close personal relationships in his discipling ministry. He needed a small support group around him as he faced the cross. Just before he went to pray, he revealed his deep inner feelings to Peter, James, and John (Matt. 26:36–38).

God's pattern of working through groups of people. Hananiah, Mishael, and Azariah banded together to maintain their relationship with the Lord and to support one another through prayer (Dan. 2:17–18). In the New Testament the early church met in homes for their spiritual growth and to reach new people for Christ (Acts 2:46).

The body concept of the church. Just as there is an interdependency among the parts of the physical body, so there is an interdependency among the members of the body of Christ. Small groups are a microcosm of the body working together.

The "one another" commands of Christ. The Bible contains numerous "one another" commands, such as, "be devoted to one another" (Rom. 12:10), "serve one another" (Gal. 5:13), "be subject to one another" (Eph. 5:21), and "encourage one another and build up one another" (1 Thess. 5:11).God's intent in these verses is to set forth a way of

life for his people that is interdependent. The best way
to give practical expression to these "one another" commands is in small groups.

Our changing family structures. The natural intergenera-
tional community, when all of the family generations
lived together, is gone. Small groups provide a parafamily
structure where people can receive the love and care they
no longer receive from families who may be fractured or
who live far away.

The disappearance of neighborhoods. In new housing tracts
the first things to go up are the privacy fences. People resist
becoming involved with neighbors but miss the feeling of
community. Small groups bring people into touch with
each other and provide a sense of accountability.

Our fragmented lives. It used to be that people developed
close relationships with people at church, in the neighborhood, and at work. Today we live such fragmented lives
that we spend little time with individuals and few people
know us completely. Small groups allow us to be known
as complete persons.

Our mobile lifestyle. Most people relocate several times in
their lifetime. As a result, people have fewer and fewer
long-term relationships. Children of mobility can make
friends fast but find it difficult to maintain lasting friendships. Small groups help us build lasting friendships that
enhance Christian growth.

Rules of Thumb for Small Groups

Whenever a congregation reaches a worship attendance of
120, it becomes increasingly difficult for the people to relate as
a family. Therefore, as a church gets larger, the congregation
must get smaller through the incorporation of small groups.
To determine how many small groups your church needs, give
some thought to the following rules of thumb.

Rule 1: A church needs seven small groups for every one hundred adults present at its Sunday morning worship services.

Rule 2: In general, 40 percent of a church's existing groups should be less than two years old. This is necessary because groups tend to be closed to the addition of newcomers twelve to eighteen months after their formation. Therefore, additional groups are crucial to the assimilation of new people.

Rule 3: Even with the best small-group ministry available, not all of your adults will choose to participate. Generally a healthy church will have 50 percent of its adult worshipers participating in its small groups.

Tips for a Good Beginning

Educate leaders. Take time to educate leaders concerning the need for a small-group ministry in your church. If your church has never used small groups before or perhaps has had a bad experience with them, plan on taking three to five years to build a solid base of commitment before beginning your small groups.

Evaluate your present ministry. Using the rules of thumb above, evaluate your church's current small-group ministry. How many small groups are already functioning? How many years have they been in existence? How many adults are participating?

Set some goals. Based on the findings of your evaluation, set some goals. For example, how many new small groups do you need? How many of your worshipers would you like to see involved? How many small-group leaders do you need to train?

Do some research. Read some books, attend seminars, and visit other churches that are successfully using small groups. Familiarize yourself with what is and isn't working in small-group ministry today.

Develop your vision. Write out a vision for a small-group ministry in your church. What is the biblical reason for small groups? Why are small groups important to your church's future? How many small groups do you hope to start in the next five years? How will small groups fit with other church ministries, such as Sunday school?

Pray for leaders. Take time to pray for potential small-group leaders in your church. Remember that before Jesus selected the twelve disciples, he spent the entire night in prayer (Luke 6:12–13).

Select potential leaders. Refuse to select people who are already involved in leadership. Look for people who are "potential" leaders and use small groups as an entry point for raising up new leaders.

29

STARTING SMALL GROUPS

There are many ways to begin a small-group ministry in a local church, and most can be categorized under one of two models—the slow-track model or the fast-track model.

The Slow-Track Model

The slow-track model is a careful and cautious approach to starting a small-group ministry. This model is best for churches that

- have attempted small groups unsuccessfully
- have a fear of small-group ministry
- have few leaders with small-group experience

The Process

Start the process with education. As a rule of thumb, take at least one year to prepare people for your future small-group ministry. If your church has an aversion to small groups, plan on taking three to five years.

Enlist a core of potential leaders. Make a list of all the people (couples and singles) who show potential leadership ability. Your list should include twice as many names as you hope to actually recruit for your first training group.

Share your vision for small groups. Schedule a meeting with each couple or single person on your list. Share with them your vision for a small-group ministry. Express your interest in training them to begin their own small group.

Train your potential leaders. Train your potential leaders in sixteen weekly sessions. At each session, spend the first forty-five minutes leading your training group in an actual small group. After a fifteen-minute break, spend the final forty-five minutes training them in small-group leadership skills.

Develop individual prospect lists. During the twelfth week of training, ask the potential leaders to make a list of people whom they will invite to be in the small group they each will start. During the last four weeks of training, teach them how to recruit people for their small group.

Begin new small groups. It is crucial that the new small groups begin the week immediately after your last training session. The more time that goes by the less likely it is that new groups will be successfully started.

Offer continuing encouragement. Call each of your new small-group leaders weekly to offer encouragement and answer questions. Host a monthly meeting for all the new small-group leaders for mutual support and sharing of ideas.

Repeat the process. Once your new small-group leaders are functioning well, repeat the process. Select another group of ten to twelve potential leaders and train them in the same manner.

Advantages of the Slow-Track Model

There are several advantages to using the slow-track model for developing small groups.

- Two training groups can be successfully completed in a normal year.
- Ten to twelve new groups can be started on a yearly basis with about an 80 percent success rate.
- The small-group ministry is developed slowly and carefully.

The Fast-Track Model

The fast-track model is a way to begin a small-group ministry quickly. This model is best for churches that

- have small-group leaders with experience
- have established a vision for small groups
- have a strong desire for small groups

The Process

Start the process with education. Spend a minimum of one year preparing your congregation for small groups. Relate the need for small groups to your church's vision and purpose. Share the benefits of participation in small groups.

Enlist and train a core of leaders. Encourage anyone who is interested in leading a small group to sign up for a one-day training session. Because most of the interested leaders will have had small-group experience, an initial training period that is shorter than that used for the slow-track model will suffice During this training session for all interested leaders, share your vision for small groups, give guidelines for leading one, and provide instruction on basic small-group leadership skills. Continue to have a monthly training session after the groups begin.

Design a variety of small groups. Allow each small-group leader to design his or her small group, following these guidelines:

- The group must be doctrinally sound.
- The group must be biblical.
- The group must be legal.
- The group must be ethical.
- The group leaders must attend a monthly leaders training session.

Advertise in advance. About six weeks prior to beginning your small groups, let people know when they can sign up and when the groups will begin. List all the available small groups, noting the meeting times, locations, leaders, and other important information.

Have a sign-up Sunday. Select a specific Sunday for the congregation to sign up for a group. If possible, have all small-group leaders seated at tables in a fellowship hall, in the gymnasium, or on the church lawn, so that interested people can talk to the leaders and sign up for a group. Limit each group to ten to twelve participants.

Begin your new groups. Begin all new groups the very next week following the sign-ups. The longer the wait before the groups begin the less successful they will be. Call each small-group leader the day after his or her group meets to give encouragement and support.

Require a regular report. Each small-group leader must turn in a regular report to a selected church leader. Groups that meet weekly report weekly, and groups that meet monthly report monthly. The report should be short, including attendance, praises, and concerns. The *attendance* figures let your church know the participation level. The *praises* give you information for advertising. The *concerns* let you know topics that future training sessions must address.

Offer continuing education. Require all small-group leaders to recruit an assistant leader. These assistant leaders should attend the monthly small-group leaders training event. As these assistants gain experience, use them to begin new groups.

Advantages of the Fast-Track Model

There are several advantages to the fast-track model.

- Numerous groups can be successfully started in a short span of time.
- A large number of people can participate in a variety of different groups.
- The small-group ministry is controlled by a system of training and reporting.

30

A Small-Group Life Cycle

We are all familiar with the basic human life cycle: birth, growth, maturity, decline, and death. In a similar way, a small group has a life cycle. By understanding the normal sequence of group development, leaders can design the activities of the group to address and resolve the specific issues found at each stage. Thus the group can develop more smoothly than might normally be the case.

Dream Stage

The first stage of the small-group life cycle is the *dream stage*. During this stage someone develops a dream to begin a small group. Then the dream is shared with others with as much detail as possible at this early stage. Finally, initial commitment to at least meet once to discuss the possibility is secured.

Technically this stage is referred to as the pre-contract stage, and there is no commitment beyond the initial interest. The small group is just in the idea or dream stage, but this stage is crucial to the successful beginning of a small group. If initial excitement and interest are not developed, it is likely that the small group will never come into being.

Decision Stage

The second stage is the *decision stage*. This takes place at the very first meeting of the small group. It is at this meeting that ideas are shared, full discussion takes place, and a final decision is made on whether to continue as a small group. Key elements of the small group are determined in this first meeting; for example, the time and place to meet, the norms of the group, the type and style of group, the purpose of the group, and how leadership will function.

In the technical language of small-group development, this is called the contract or covenant stage. It is during this first meeting that a contract is agreed on that will govern the small group in its future meetings.

Delegation Stage

The third stage is the *delegation stage*. It is during this stage that roles, functions, expectations, and agendas are sorted out. Some small-group leaders refer to this period of time as "power and control," since many issues must be determined before the group can become cohesive and bond together. This period of time is not necessarily an angry time but more of a shaking down of ideas, expectations, and procedures.

The delegation stage is a period of conflict that, if handled well, leads to a cohesive group. Yet, if the group never is able to reach a common understanding of roles and goals, then the group may never bond. If a group continues to lack a sense of togetherness or bonding beyond four or five meetings, it is likely that issues during the delegation stage have not been resolved.

Dedication Stage

The fourth stage is the *dedication stage*. At this stage a small group reaches the point where the members have bonded. There will be a sense of harmony and cohesiveness among group members. The resistance felt during the delegation stage will have gone away. Group procedures are agreed on, roles are defined, and personal opinions are openly expressed. During the dedication stage, decisions are made with the full cooperation of all members. Group energy is focused on fulfilling the goals of the group. Problems are solved and tasks are efficiently performed.

This is the most difficult stage for any group to achieve, but it reflects what most people want in a small-group experience. In essence, the dedication stage is when group members trust each other enough to share, laugh, and cry together.

Decline Stage

The fifth stage is the *decline stage*. As in all life cycles, a period of decline is to be expected. Even in the best small groups, the dedication stage will normally not last more than twelve to eighteen months before it begins to dissolve. This is a normal process and should not be interpreted as a negative aspect of small-group development.

New problems in the group are often indicators that the group has entered into the decline stage. First, people may begin showing up late for group meetings. Second, if work is to be completed outside of small group meetings, such as a Bible study, people may come to meetings with it incomplete. Third, there may be an increase in conflict between group members. It may actually feel like the group has reverted to the delegation stage. If so, it is a likely signal that the group has entered the decline stage. At this point the wise small-group leader will call for a meeting to discuss the future of the small group. The entire group should decide if they want to continue on together in the same manner or change directions.

Dead-End Stage

The sixth stage is the *dead-end stage*. The small group enters this stage when they decide they cannot continue on together without some changes. They have literally reached a dead end and must make fresh decisions about the future.

In some cases a small group may continue to meet and function with ever increasing difficulty. They are actually at a dead end but just won't admit it. This occurs when a group has bonded closely together and experienced a very supportive dedication stage. Each knows in his or her heart that the group as it now functions has run its course, but each is unwilling to face this fact publicly. The love and support they feel for one another is so strong that they hate to think of parting.

Determination Stage

The last stage is the *determination stage*. Three possibilities exist for a group that enters this stage. First, the group might decide to develop a new dream—set new goals or begin a new type of group. In this situation the group members often continue to meet, but the direction of the group is changed. A few members may decide not to continue meeting, and a few new members may be invited to join.

Second, the group might decide to multiply and form two or three different small groups. People's needs and the speed of their personal growth vary from one person to another. Groups that functioned well should see the personal growth of each member as an indication of its success. Likewise, the multiplying of one or two new groups is an expression of the success of the group.

Third, the group may decide to disband. If this is the decision, it is important that the group meet for one last time to wrap things up. Don't ever disband without taking the time to bring a sense of closure to the group. After spending time together, it is wise to allow members to express their appreciation and love to each other.

PERSONAL DEVELOPMENT

31

THE NEED TO READ

Keeping up with our reading is essential to effective ministry in the twenty-first century, but many of us find that there's just too much to read. For instance, the average American reads three thousand notices, one hundred newspapers, and thirty-six magazines in one year. Large newsstands commonly offer a choice of more than twenty-five hundred different magazines. More than ten thousand different periodicals are published in the United States each year. Printed information doubles every four to five years.

This large amount of information creates a disorder brought about by our detail-saturated, paper-polluted, information-mad society, characterized by an obsessive-compulsive tendency to read everything about everything. When the amount of reading matter ingested exceeds the amount of energy available for digestion, the surplus accumulates and is converted by stress and overstimulation into the unhealthy state known as IOA (information overload anxiety).

Being a Discerning Reader

Time spent reading books, journals, and magazines that don't pertain to our life and ministry is a waste of time. It adds to our guilt of not being able to keep up with it all. Here are some ideas for handling this information glut and the guilt we feel when we can't read it all.

Realize it is impossible to know everything. Even if you were able to read every journal, book, and periodical available, you still wouldn't know it all. In fact you wouldn't know as much about your world as Galileo or Aristotle knew about theirs. It would simply be too much information to remember. So relax and focus on the ideas that follow.

Determine the reading that is germane to your work. Instead of trying to read everything that you think you should, determine what is essential. List the books, magazines, and journals that are directly related to your work and interests. Narrow your list down to the germane.

Use vicarious readers. Ask two or three people to read for you. You read what you have decided is germane and ask your readers to read material in other areas, passing along to you copies of quotations or articles that might be significant to your work.

Select reading based on reading lists. Ask respected leaders in your fields of interest to recommend ten books and articles for your reading. Then, until you have more time, limit your reading to items found on their lists.

Use the shard method. Purchase the magazines, newspapers, or journals you think look interesting. Let them stack up on a shelf until they reach the shelf above. Then take the time to skim through them, tearing out the articles that strike you as important to your life and ministry. Throw the rest away. The shards, then, will be meaningful reading for you. Waiting and going through all the periodicals at once is more efficient than trying to page through each one as it arrives.

Scan—don't read. Avoid trying to read everything word for word. Develop the habit of scanning the headlines and skimming articles. Stop to read thoroughly only those articles or books that seem key to your ministry.

Practice the ambush technique. Listen to what your colleagues say are the best books, articles, newsletters, and journals to read. After you've heard the same one recommended repeatedly, then ambush or attack it by reading only that one book, article, newsletter, or journal.

A Leader Reads

An old adage says that leaders are readers. John Kenneth Galbraith said that only those who have the right information, the strategic knowledge, and the handy facts could make it in the last quarter of the twentieth century. This is even more true in the fast-paced twenty-first century.

It's obvious that you as a leader need to read, but you will need to trim your reading diet so that you have time to acquire the information that is essential for your effective leadership and ministry.

32

PERSONAL TIME MANAGEMENT

Learning how to manage our personal time begins with dispelling some of the myths of time management.

Myth: You need more time.
Truth: You have all the time you need for what God wants you to do.

Myth: You have less time than others.
Truth: You have the same amount of time as the busiest person.

Myth: You can save time.
Truth: You cannot store up time; it keeps moving.

Myth: You can manage time.
Truth: You can manage only yourself.

Myth: You can accomplish more by working longer.
Truth: You must work smarter not longer.

Myth: You can make up lost time.
Truth: You can never regain lost time.

Myth: You are too busy to do all you have to do.
Truth: You have time to do all you should do.

Time Wasters

A survey of twenty-five Christian executives found the greatest time wasters to be the following.

- looking for misplaced items
- unexpected visitors
- unanticipated interruptions
- unnecessary correspondence
- poor organization
- waiting for people
- reading material not relevant to the job
- lack of preparation
- delayed responses to correspondence
- telephone calls
- coffee breaks
- failure to delegate
- writing long letters

A similar survey of pastors found that their major time wasters were the following.

- *Fire fighting.* Dealing with problems as they arise, rather than planning ahead, is ineffective.

- *Interruptions.* The majority of these time wasters were related to unexpected phone calls and visitors.
- *Daydreaming.* Failure to live in the present becomes a time waster when hours are spent on introspection (reviewing the past) and dreaming (fantasizing about the future).
- *Procrastination.* Time is wasted when decisions and work that need to be done are delayed. One pastor noted, "I was going to preach on procrastination, but I put it off."
- *Poor communication.* Time is wasted when we fail to make clear what we want done, where to meet, or when things are needed.

Twenty Ideas for Effective Use of Time

1. Pray for the wisdom to use time effectively (Ps. 90:12).
2. Establish a routine and follow it (Eccles. 3:1).
3. Schedule tasks on a calendar.
4. Eliminate tasks you don't have to do.
5. Delegate tasks to others (Exod. 18:13–26).
6. Use time in large blocks. Working on a project in one chunk of sixty minutes is better than working on it in twelve chunks of five minutes each.
7. Practice efficient reading habits. Read reviews, skim books and articles, and ask others to read for you.
8. Practice wastebasketry—throw things away before they can clutter your desk.
9. Learn how to terminate unproductive phone calls.
10. Speed up your decision making, realizing you will never have all the information you want.
11. Set long-range goals.
12. Do the hard things first. If you have to eat a lot of frogs, eat the big ones first.
13. Do difficult tasks in phases. Eighty percent of the task is usually completed in the first phase.
14. Use a committee of two. Decisions are made more quickly when few people are involved.

15. Answer correspondence quickly. Scribble a response on the original letter.
16. Handle correspondence only once. Use it, file it, or throw it away.
17. Allow your secretary to make appointments for you and answer correspondence with form letters.
18. Hold meetings in other people's offices, so you can leave when you're ready.
19. Stand up for meetings. The meetings will be shorter.
20. Hold meetings thirty minutes before quitting time.

33

Hooked on Learning

Once upon a time seminary education prepared a pastor for a lifetime of ministry. The very word *seminary* comes from the Latin *seminarius* meaning "of seed." The concept buried deep in the word suggests that seminary education is the seed that will grow into a lifetime of ministry.

For many years a seminary education did just that. It prepared students for a lifelong ministry. Of course, that all changed in the middle of the twentieth century.

Church leaders are quite familiar with many of the changes that have taken place in ministry. As one pastor commented in a seminar, "I'm faced with codependency, divorce recovery, blended families, and all kinds of physical and emotional abuse. Seminary didn't prepare me for this. I need help!"

Life and ministry are changing at such a rapid pace that it no longer makes sense to assume a three- or four-year seminary education can provide the seed for a lifetime of ministry. The new learning paradigm that must be implemented today is lifelong learning.

Lifelong Learning

The first thing we need to understand is that there are three basic types of learning.

Type A: Maintenance learning. Maintenance learning is the acquisition of fixed methods, rules, and processes for known and recurring situations. This type of learning is foundational but quickly becomes outdated when methods, rules, and processes change.

Type B: Innovative learning. Innovative learning works best in times of turbulence and change. It fosters change and renewal and helps one think through problems. Emergencies, adversities, or catastrophes often stimulate innovative learning. This "learning by shock" prepares individuals and organizations to face the present and the future, but most often it is reactionary.

Type C: Anticipatory learning. Anticipatory learning prepares the individual and organization to be proactive not reactive. It involves thinking about possible contingencies and long-range alternatives. Forecasting, simulations, scenarios, and models are used to shield us from the trauma of learning by shock. They each allow us to think through potential situations, foreseeing pros and cons before the actual events take place.

To keep up these days, leaders must move beyond maintenance and innovative learning to anticipatory learning.

Tips for Lifelong Learners

To be a lifelong learner is to be a beginner. While we may at first think that a beginner is one who is not knowledgeable, educated, or an expert, this is not what I have in mind. A true beginner is a person who has the ability to see the world with fresh eyes. A beginner sees day-to-day situations with eyes that are open to learn more about his or her world.

Lifelong learners take to heart what Albert Einstein said: "The more I learn, the more I realize I don't know, and the more I realize I don't know, the more I want to learn."

Lifelong learning is more about attitude than action. A lifelong learner learns through every event—good or bad, every success or failure. A lifelong learner learns through every relationship—friend or foe.

We must learn how to learn, how to acquire the necessary knowledge, creativity, and action steps to anticipate and then handle problems in our particular ministries. The more we are open to learn the more we are prepared to reshape our ministries for fruitful tomorrows.

How do we become lifelong learners? Here are a few tips suggested by fellow learners:

Be aware of the "resistance factor." As humans we get caught up in the web of present involvement and resist looking at the future. Being entangled in dealing with the *now* causes us to ignore the possibilities on the horizon. Overcome this resistance by becoming hooked on learning.

Stop blaming others. When we look for someone or something to blame for what happens in our ministry, we use up a lot of energy, and most often we don't learn from the experience. Instead of seeking to find fault, identify the issue and ask yourself: *What can I learn from this situation?*

Take personal responsibility. A lifelong learner accepts his or her responsibility to understand and learn from every situation. The intent of a lifelong learner is to learn about himself or herself, others, and the situation by asking three key questions:

- What part did I play in this situation?
- What part did others play in this situation?
- What can I learn about this situation?

Be courageous. Someone once noted that there are only two life paths—the path of dread and the path of courage. People who follow the path of dread protect themselves from learning by shying away from any situation that might cause them discomfort or pain. Those who choose the path of courage willingly experience temporary discouragement, discomfort, or failure to learn more about themselves, others, and situations.

Be aware of learning situations. Relationships help you learn about yourself and others. Obstacles become stepping-stones to greater understanding. Failures offer adventures to be overcome. In short, almost every situation is a learning opportunity.

Plan on formal quarterly training. Set a goal to attend some form of training seminar, class, or workshop every three months. Continual training will not only keep you abreast of current trends but energized about your ministry. It is essential not only that you stay on top of what is happening in your field but that you learn and grow.

Commit to lifelong learning. One leader noted: "Only to the extent that you grow does your life really become fulfilled. Stop growing and you will, for all practical purposes, stop living."

PART 12

PLANNING

34

TRAINING A CHURCH
BOARD

There was a day when the average layperson did not want to get involved with decision making. After all, that is what the church paid the pastor to do for them. Today, however, most of our churches have volunteers who are fully engaged and active in the detailed activities of their church.

But how does a pastor ensure that those who are making the decisions do so with the right biblical foundation, motives, and understanding? The answer is training.

Here are some essential components of a training program for the local church board:

> *Biblical job description.* Over the many years of church history, the job description of a church board member has changed. Walk your members through a clear presentation of what an elder, deacon, and/or deaconess is supposed to do. When they were selected, they were asked to serve—not supervise!

The mission statement. Each board member should understand, agree with, and be able to recite the church mission statement. Since it contains the reason for your church's existence, the statement is something that leaders must know and buy into.

Church structure. As dry as organizational charts can be, they are essential for smooth communication and accountability. Each board member needs to know who is responsible for what and who reports to whom. Without this understanding, you will have chaos and confusion.

Building team ministry. It does not come naturally for a group of people to function as a team. Creating a genuine team dynamic is more than simply forming a group. This is especially true in ministry, where the motivational techniques, such as a paycheck, used in corporate settings are absent.

Effective leadership in ministry. An important fact that the board needs to understand is that the qualities of leadership are more important than styles. The heart of the leader is of more importance to God than the power he or she possesses.

Planning and goal setting. Those in leadership need to know the obstacles to long- and short-range planning, for example, how to answer people who believe planning is unbiblical. It is both biblical and mandatory that a church formulate plans for the future.

Resolving interpersonal conflicts. In a recent national survey, 85 percent of pastors said they called on church board members to help them resolve interpersonal conflicts in the church. Knowing how to do this biblically requires some instruction.

Modeling a biblical lifestyle. Since most people in a church assume that those serving diligently in a position of spiritual leadership must be growing in their personal walk with the Lord, board members may be tempted to appear more spiritual than they really are. It is critical to the life of the church that board members have an authentic walk with God.

Dealing with financial storms. The need for responsible financial stewardship has never been more obvious than in the past few years. The ups and downs of the economy have made it obvious that sound financial planning is a necessity. The church board is usually at the center of issues related to church finances, and the board members must receive guidance in proper financial management.

Filling the empty pulpit. Few decisions affect the life of the church as much as the selection of its shepherd. Board members need instruction in the timing, process, and details of this most crucial leadership responsibility.

Moral and ethical dilemmas. Without doubt, one of the hardest challenges a board member may have to face is dealing with immorality or unethical conduct within the congregation. Few other issues will create as much emotional pain, stress, and soul-searching as dealing with such problems. Educate leaders on how to handle violations of this type before such a situation arises.

Legal issues in the church. Church board members have been entrusted with the responsibility of overseeing certain matters that could have legal impact on the church. Knowing how to handle issues of licensing, taxes, and liability risk require training and guidance.

Gossips, complainers, and constant nitpickers. Regardless of one's position in the church, denominational affiliation, years of experience, gender, level of education, or age, the one common denominator of leadership is that you will face rumors, complaints, and opposition. Board members need help learning how to cope with these inevitable pressures.

Bringing renewal to the church. There is much that a board can do to encourage or inhibit church growth. A wise pastor will educate the board about these issues.

35

FAITH PLANNING

We are all interested in the direction of our church in the coming years. It is our desire to be sensitive to God's leading for our church, realizing that "the mind of man plans his way, but the LORD directs his steps" (Prov. 16:9).

God, of course, is the greatest planner. From the beginning he has carefully been working out his plan to redeem the creation and lost mankind. To Abraham, God revealed part of his plan by declaring, "I will make you a great nation, and I will bless you, and make your name great; and so you shall be a blessing" (Gen. 12:2).

Later Paul explained to Timothy that Jesus Christ "gave Himself as a ransom for all, the testimony given at the proper time" (1 Tim. 2:6).

A Faith Planning Model

One model for faith planning involves five distinct steps.

Step 1: Faith planning begins by seeking God's guidance and direction. In faith we turn our hearts and minds toward God in prayer, seeking his guidance and direction for the future.

Step 2: Faith planning continues by clarifying the vision of what God wants done in our ministry situation. By looking at our past experiences (successes and failures), our present opportunities (needs of people in our community), and our current resources (people, money, and time), God leads us to determine our priorities for today's and tomorrow's ministry.

Step 3: Faith planning takes God's vision and puts it into terms that are accomplishable and measurable. Determining precisely what, when, where, and by whom the plan will be done is crucial to fulfill the faith plan.

Step 4: Faith planning considers the resources that are available to do the job. What are the available resources in terms of people, money, time, prayer, and commitment?

Step 5: Faith planning honestly evaluates how effectively the plan is implemented. Are we doing what we planned to do? Why or why not?

Developing a Faith Plan

Begin the development of your faith plan by organizing a task force comprised of people who will be responsible for developing the plan. Choose people who care deeply about your church and the work of God in the world and your community. Be sure to include some new people who have attended your church less than two years.

Take time to examine the purpose of your church. Why does your church exist? What does the Bible indicate your church should be doing? If you already have a purpose statement, reconfirm your commitment to it. Or, if you do not have a purpose statement, write one.

Spend some time listing the real needs of people in your church's community, and dream about how your church's purpose statement might be expressed in practical terms to meet some of those needs. Write and rewrite your ideas into a practical statement of your vision for the future.

Establish some faith goals that will take you from where you are today to fulfillment of your vision. Faith goals should be specific, measurable, and practical in that they will help your vision become a reality.

The Ingredients

A good long-range plan will include a review and/or writing of the following four basic statements.

1. *A statement of your purpose.* A purpose or mission statement is the biblical reason your church exists.

   - It should be founded clearly on God's Word.
   - It must be communicated so that people know what it means.

   Key: Normally a purpose statement is expressed in fewer than twenty-five words.

2. *A statement of your vision.* A vision statement tells how you expect to work out your purpose in your ministry area.

   - It must be relevant to your place of ministry.
   - It must be large enough to challenge people but small enough not to discourage them.

   Key: The vision statement answers the question, If our church could be all that God wants it to be in the next five years, what would we be doing?

3. *A statement of your values.* A values statement is a listing of the principles that drive your church.

- Your values are the hidden factors behind all decisions.
- They are key to an effective ministry.

Key: Values are often emotionally rooted in the life history of a church.

4. *A statement of your goals.* A statement of goals is an enlargement of a church's purpose and vision, explaining in detail what must take place to accomplish them.

- Goals detail how your particular church hopes to fulfill its purpose.
- They are best seen in your church's programs.

Key: Goals relate directly to each major ministry area.

The statement of your goals will be the longest section of your plan and should outline what you hope to achieve in each major area of ministry. Most churches will list goals in at least the following areas.

- education
- worship
- outreach
- assimilation
- finances
- facilities
- missions
- adult ministry
- youth ministry
- children's ministry

You may need to add areas to this section for special ministries, such as a Christian school.

The Process

Recognizing that it is not possible to list all the ideas and dreams that members may suggest, the planning process seeks to note the ones your church must begin to emphasize in the next few years.

Step 1: Begin with the senior pastor. The pastor should write a brief statement for each of the above four ingredients, noting ideas that he believes are particularly important to the future direction of your church.

Step 2: Review with associate staff. Write a rough outline of the pastor's ideas and ask each staff person to review them, adding their own insights and comments.

Step 3: Review with church leaders. Blend the comments from the staff with those of the pastor and give copies to each person on your main leadership board, with the request that they add their own ideas.

Step 4: Review with ministry leaders. Ask two or three leaders from every major ministry area in your church to review the developing plan and add their ideas to it.

Step 5: Write the first rough draft. After the information has been received from the ministry leaders in step 4, have the long-range planning team meet to compile and write a complete rough draft of your long-range plan.

Step 6: Survey the congregation. Once a rough draft has been written, take the pulse of the congregation by giving copies to church members for review and comments.

Step 7: Compile a final draft. After taking the pulse of the congregation, write a final draft of your long-range plan and move through whatever process is appropriate to get it approved.

Remember that your plan will go through several rewrites before it is finally accepted. The normal length of time to develop a long-range plan is six to twelve months.

Once the plan is finalized and approved, it must be communicated appropriately to the entire congregation. Consider holding a State of the Church day when the long-range plan can be presented to the congregation. Providing the congregation with written communication explaining the plan along with a spoken presentation may also be helpful.

36

LOOK FOR YOUR STARS

Most of us have experienced a time when a new understanding or insight surprised us so suddenly that we almost shouted "a-ha!" This happened to me a number of years ago when I was pastor of a church in Southern California. Five new couples were sitting in a circle in my office for a new members' class. The couples had recently been won to the Lord by two families in the church and were now taking steps toward membership.

During the class, we discussed the gospel, a few key doctrines, and the need for baptism and membership in a community of believers. While looking around the circle, I was stunned by the realization that just two families in my church were responsible for all ten of these new converts. Ten new converts at one time was super, but the fact that only two families were directly responsible for them was an eye-opening "a-ha" experience for me.

Later on, further research revealed that the same two families could be tied to almost all the new converts our church had seen during the previous three years.

The 80/20 Rule

What I had discovered in my "a-ha" experience was the Pareto Principle: 80 percent of your results come from 20 percent of your effort—commonly called the 80/20 rule.

I've since learned that this principle may be broken down even further as follows.

20 percent effort equals 80 percent results.

30 percent effort equals 15 percent results.

50 percent effort equals 5 percent results.

In evangelism this means 20 percent of your members will win 80 percent of your converts, 30 percent of your members will win 15 percent of your converts, and 50 percent of your members will win 5 percent of your converts.

In giving this means that 20 percent of your members will give 80 percent of the money, 30 percent of your members will give 15 percent of the money, and 50 percent of your members will give 5 percent of the money.

In ministries this means that 20 percent of your ministries will attract 80 percent of your people, 30 percent of your ministries will attract 15 percent of your people, and 50 percent of your ministries will attract 5 percent of your people.

This principle demands serious thought.

Thinking It Through

At first, this principle may not seem that important. Yet the more you think it through, the more you will begin to understand its strategic implications. The following chart will help you visualize the impact of your effort on the end results.

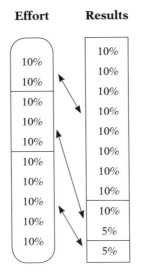

Effort   Results

Looking at the chart from left to right reveals that only a little of what you do produces much in the way of results. For example, time invested in only 20 percent of your activities is usually multiplied fourfold in end results.

Looking at the chart from right to left reveals how to invest your resources of time, energy, money, and people. For example, to get the best results, you should invest 80 percent of your resources in the 20 percent of the programs, priorities, and people that are the most effective.

In this day of limited ministry resources, it's crucial that you put your time, energy, money, and people where they will do the most good.

Concentrate on Your Stars

A lot of what you read about leadership and church growth is sound advice. However, seldom do you hear this effective strategy: Concentrate on your stars.

A careful look at your church will reveal that a limited number of people, programs, and priorities are causing your church to move forward. To make the most of the resources of your church, consider the following.

> *Identify your top programs.* Make a list of all the ministries and programs your church offers. Then, beside each one, note how many people each ministry touches. Which ministries are in the top 20 percent?
>
> *Identify your top leaders.* Make a list of all your leaders or influential people. Then, rewrite the list ranking them according to their level of influence in your church. Who falls into the top 20 percent?
>
> *Identify your top priorities.* Make a list of all the things you need to do each week. Then prioritize them according to how crucial each is to the growth of your church. Which priorities fall into the top 20 percent?
>
> *Identify your top goals.* Make a list of all the goals your church has established for this year. Once again, rank them in order, starting with those that are most likely to help your church grow spiritually and numerically. Which goals then fall into the top 20 percent?
>
> *Identify your top outreach producers.* Make two lists of all the people and programs that have resulted in individuals coming to Christ and/or into your church over the last three years. Who are the people in the top 20 percent? Which programs fall into the top 20 percent?

Your *stars* in each case are the people and programs in the top 20 percent. To be a good steward and to see better results, focus 80 percent of your time, energy, money, and training on your stars.

PART 13

MANAGEMENT

37

TO COUNT
OR NOT TO COUNT

Pastors and church leaders often have an aversion to keeping records. Some express the feeling that churches should not be in the "numbers game." Others fear that keeping records will lead to pride and an unholy trust in statistics.

Numbers, though, are not necessarily evil. The writer of Acts carefully communicated the growth of the early church using records and statistics. From 120 persons (Acts 1:15) the early church grew to 3,000 (2:41), and then added another 5,000 men (4:4). When the numbers expanded, the growth was recorded as simply "multitudes of men and women" (5:14).

Consider also the parable of the lost sheep in Luke 15. The shepherd left the ninety-nine sheep in the open field to look for the one that was lost. But how did the shepherd know one sheep was lost? Obviously he had counted them.

Reporting statistics is an acceptable and useful means of recording the results of evangelism and shepherding church members. It is not a numbers game but a way to evaluate our faithfulness to Christ's commission to seek and save the lost.

The Value of Statistics

When we go to a doctor's office, a nurse carefully records our temperature, blood pressure, weight, height, heartbeat, and other statistically measured factors. Using these statistics, the doctor then formulates a judgment about our health. In no way, of course, do such measurements heal us. However, they are an objective way to gauge our health.

Similarly, keeping accurate ministry records gives us an objective understanding of the health of our church. While statistics certainly do not lead anyone to Christ or cause anyone to grow in the Lord, they do assist us in understanding where, when, and how our ministry is most effective. For example, a church may work hard at attracting new people to church yet fail to incorporate the people into the life of the church. By carefully watching the attendance pattern of newer members, it is easy to see which people are becoming involved in the church and which are not, allowing for an appropriate response.

Records to Keep

Church leaders who desire to increase the effectiveness of their ministry will find it helpful to keep certain records. You should know:

What attracts people to your church. Few churches know why they attract people. Asking newcomers how they heard about your church and carefully recording their answers will produce a picture of what attracts people to your church and enable you to focus more of your efforts in that direction.

What keeps people in your church. People stay in a church if they build friendships, join a small group, and find a place to serve. Tracking all new members to see if they are involved in these three ways will help assimilate the fruits of your outreach efforts.

Why people become members of your church. People join a
church through conversion, transfer of membership, and
being born into it. Tracing these means over three years
allows you to see where your church's outreach is strongest
and where it needs to be improved.

How people find Christ in your church. Interviewing new
converts to find out how they made commitments to Christ
will highlight the ministries and individuals who are most
effective in winning new converts.

How often people attend your church. Charting your church's
worship attendance will establish a trend line of your
church's development and spotlight currents of change
so that you can make appropriate adjustments in your
ministry strategy.

Getting the Data

Gathering data can be accomplished in several ways. The
most common methods include the following.

- *Interviews.* A phone call to guests within twenty-four hours
  of their visit to your church is a personal touch that allows for a brief exchange of information. In fact recent
  studies have found that new people are willing to give out
  more information in a phone interview than by any other
  means.

- *A guest book.* A guest book is the least reliable source for
  information about people who attend your church. Many
  people simply pass it by, and, since the guest book is only
  for visitors, regular attenders have no way to indicate their
  attendance.

- *Attendance cards.* Cards work best when everyone attending is asked to sign them—members and guests—and the
  platform leader makes a big point about them.

- *Friendship pads.* An effective way of taking attendance for
  most churches is a pad of paper—with places for name,

address, and telephone number—that is passed down each row of seats. Each person fills it in and passes it to the next person. It is then passed back to where it began, allowing each person to see the names of those sitting in the row.

- *Mundane record keeping.* Membership, Sunday school, and other participation records will highlight potential problem areas before it is too late.

Records are most accurate when kept on a weekly basis but if that seems a bit much, keep records during the months of October and May and project your findings to the total year, as these two months tend to give the most accurate statistics.

Keeping good records will aid your church in successfully fulfilling its part in the Great Commission.

38

THE 80 PERCENT RULE

The voice on the other end of the phone sounded perplexed. "How come we can't seem to grow larger than one hundred people?" asked the pastor.

As the conversation continued, I learned that, during the pastor's fifteen-year tenure, his church had experienced three different years when the worship attendance averaged above one hundred. However, in each case the church couldn't maintain the higher attendance and it dropped back below one hundred the following year.

Further research revealed that the peaks and valleys of attendance came in patterns. One year the church averaged 115 worshipers. But then worship attendance dropped to an average of 84 worshipers during the following three years before it once again rose to 105. Then the same attendance pattern was repeated.

While visiting a Sunday morning worship service, I estimated that the pews would comfortably seat about one hundred people. The answer to the pastor's question was fairly obvious. The church was experiencing the "80 percent rule of thumb."

Win Arn labeled this the "87:100 worship attendance ratio." It means that "when 87 of every 100 seats are filled on an average Sunday morning, worship attendance will begin to plateau" (Win Arn, *The Church Growth Ratio Book*, Pasadena: Church Growth,1987). The rule holds true in all sizes of churches—small, medium, or large.

Understanding the Basics

Though the 80 percent rule may be a fairly well-known concept of church ministry, it may be helpful to consider some of the basics.

The 80 percent rule is based on a church's weekly average worship attendance. To calculate this most accurately, average the worship attendance of every Sunday in a given year. In this way the high attendance on some Sundays balances out the low attendance on others and gives an accurate picture of worship attendance.

The 80 percent rule is based on the total number of seats available to the congregation. Seats in the choir loft or on the platform are not to be used in the total count, and only one-half of the seats in a balcony should be counted. Carefully observe the number of people who usually sit in a full pew and use that number in calculating seating capacity.

The 80 percent rule is based on the ratio of attendance to total seats available. Once you know your average worship attendance per Sunday for a given year, divide that number by the total number of available seats. For example, an average worship attendance of 150 divided by 200 available seats equals a 75:100 ratio.

Our Need for Space

A number of years ago anthropologist Edward T. Hall conducted a pioneering study on the effects of physical distance on personal interactions. He found four main body-space zones: *intimate*, *personal*, *social*, and *public*.

The *public zone* is the distance at which pastors, teachers, and lecturers most often stand in relation to their audience, usually a space of twelve feet or more between speaker and listener.

The *social zone* is the distance we often stand apart from each other when talking in a small group. This zone is between four and twelve feet and is suitable for fairly impersonal exchanges, such as meetings or interviews.

The *personal zone*—between eighteen inches and four feet of another person—approaches normal touching range. People often attempt to protect their personal zones by placing handbags, coats, or other barriers between themselves and others.

The *intimate zone* is the distance we use for embracing. We allow only family members or close friends into this zone. For North Americans and Europeans, any invasion by strangers into this zone causes mental and physical anxiety, irritation, and fear.

When church attendance exceeds 80 percent of the auditorium capacity, people are forced into an uncomfortably close seating arrangement. The 80 percent rule of thumb comes into play because the personal and intimate zones of worshipers are invaded.

Of course, people may tolerate this close proximity for a short while, but eventually the tension created through invasion of their personal and intimate zones forces people to avoid the situation, and so, in a church, the attendance falls as some people begin to attend less often and others depart to relieve the tension. While attendance may exceed 80 percent for a while, it will do so only temporarily.

How to Respond

There are at least seven approaches to alleviating the 80 percent problem.

Expand the seating capacity. If the space is available, a church can put in additional seats. In some cases using a different style of seat or a different arrangement can add significantly more seating to an otherwise full auditorium.

Remodel or build a new sanctuary. A sanctuary can be remodeled to add a balcony or more seating, it can be enlarged, or a new worship center can be built to accommodate the growth.

Add additional worship services. A common response to the problem of overcrowding is the use of multiple worship services on Sunday morning or evenings during the week. This approach is very cost effective, because facilities don't need to be remodeled or new ones built.

Plant a daughter church. Spinning off worshipers to plant a daughter church may temporarily relieve the overcrowding at the mother church. However, the people who leave are usually replaced within a year, and the problem presents itself once again.

Start a satellite church. An approach that should be considered more often is starting a satellite church. The church is still one church, but it meets in two or more locations.

Use overflow rooms. Establishing overflow rooms, where the service is delivered through video projection, is a good approach but most often a temporary one.

Begin house churches. Establishing house churches, which worshipers rotate in attending one Sunday a month, relieves overcrowding at the main facility by about 25 percent. Once again, this approach is a temporary stopgap measure rather than a long-term answer.

39

MANAGING CONFLICT

After I graduated from high school, I spent a short time working in a lumberyard near my home. Handling lumber all day
left a lot of annoying little splinters in my hands, which were
irritating, but they never caused me to stop work. I plucked
them out quite easily.

One day as I was working on a project for the foreman, I
inadvertently missed a nail with my hammer and struck my
thumb. The pain was so strong that I immediately dropped
the hammer and held my thumb tightly in an effort to control the pain. It was quite a while before I could return to the
project.

Working with people naturally brings out differences. The
different views and opinions that people express about ministry
are like small splinters. While they often create minor irrita-
tions, they usually do not bring ministry to a halt.

Conflict, however, has a more negative impact on ministry.
Like hitting your thumb with a hammer, it causes you to stop
and deal with the issue before you can move forward. Differ-

ences between people become conflict when the level of frustration is so great that it brings ministry to a halt.

A good rule of thumb regarding conflict states: We must manage conflict; we can never remove differences. So how can we manage conflict effectively?

Three Types of Conflict

Conflict, which means literally "to strike together," may be:

- interpersonal—conflict with people
- intrapersonal—conflict within ourselves
- substantive—conflict over issues

Here are four insights concerning the three types of conflict:

Substantive conflict generates interpersonal and intrapersonal conflict. Disagreement on issues quite often degenerates into conflict between people.

Eighty percent of church conflicts are over methods and procedures. Most conflicts arise from differences of opinion on how things are to be done rather than from the values underlying them.

People often forget the issue but remember the interpersonal conflict. Personal statements and feelings remain with people long after the issue is forgotten.

All issues are not equally important. It is best to choose carefully the battles you fight. Only on rare occasions are issues important enough to fight over.

Steps to Follow

When trying to resolve any type of conflict, follow these twelve steps:

1. *Note when differences become conflict.* Differences will always be present in a church. Pay special attention to these differences when they affect the ability to carry on ministry. It is at this point that conflict is present and must be managed.

2. *Identify the type of conflict.* Is the conflict primarily intrapersonal, interpersonal, or substantive?

3. *Identify the norms of the situation.* How are things usually done? What is acceptable behavior? What are the unwritten norms that govern such situations? For example, an unwritten norm might be a rule against taking coffee into the sanctuary.

4. *Identify the rules.* What do the constitution and bylaws dictate? What do policy manuals or traditions require?

5. *Identify the contingencies.* What is the price you will have to pay if you face the conflict? What will you lose? What do you stand to gain? Is it worth it?

6. *Identify the potential actions of others.* What have you seen the parties involved do in similar situations? What are they likely to do now? What can you predict about their behavior?

7. *Identify the values of the situation.* What ought to be done? What is right? What is biblical? What is best for the church at large?

8. *Identify the assumptions of the situation.* What are the foundational beliefs involved? What is believed to be true? What is expected? What is traditional?

9. *Identify the action to be taken.* First, identify the desired results. What would you like to see happen? Based on steps 2 through 8, what is the appropriate action to take at this time?

10. *Identify the leadership approach.* Adjust your leadership approach to fit the situation. You don't need to handle every conflict in the same way. There are five leadership approaches that may be used to deal with any conflict:

Lose/yield. Choose this approach when the relationship between people is more important than the issue. In essence the issue is not worth fighting about, so you yield on the issue to keep the relationship strong.

Win/lose. Choose this approach when the issue is more important than the relationship. In essence the issue is worth fighting about, so you try to win even if you lose the relationship. When this approach is used, you must be willing to pay the high cost of lost relationships.

Lose/lose. Rarely choose this approach since both sides lose and the conflict might ruin the church. This approach to conflict management is too severe and usually not worth the price.

Compromise. This approach is the weakest and creates a no-win situation. The conflict is never managed and no one is pleased.

Win/win. Choose this option whenever possible, because it creates positive results for both parties involved in the conflict. This approach is not always viable, which is why other approaches are often needed.

11. *Pray!* Spend time with God, asking him for insight, direction, and humility before you proceed. Ask others to pray with you for God's leading.

12. *Take action!* There comes a point at which you must take action. Because conflict disrupts the ministry of the church, you cannot allow it to continue, even if it means you cannot arrive at a win/win solution. Follow God's leading and do what must be done.

PART 14

STAFF

40

STAFFING FOR GROWTH

Throughout most of church history few churches were large enough to have multiple church staffs. It has only been since the Industrial Age of the mid-1800s that enough people were clustered in cities to produce churches large enough to need multiple staffs.

Even then multiple staffing did not become a well-known phenomenon until the last century when the growing complexity of the Information Age made it nearly impossible for a single pastor to deal with all the issues and needs of people. As the secular world moved toward specialization and subspecialization, so the church responded with specialization to effectively minister to people's complex needs.

A simple observation of the majority of churches with multiple staffs reveals, however, that many are staffed for a decline or numerical plateau rather than for growth. Fortunately, there is a model of church staffing that will aid in the growth of churches rather than contribute to their stagnation.

New Church Development

Observers of growing churches find that the best years of a church's numerical growth are often the first fifteen to twenty years of its existence. Stated another way, the fastest growing churches are new churches. To understand the suggested model of staffing, let's walk through the early years of a new church.

When a church-planting pastor goes into a new area, the first responsibility on his desk is to find some new people. This finding of new people is evangelism. Since the new pastor has no people to care for, no program to administer, and no worship service to lead, all his energy, prayer, and effort are directed toward finding new people. Thus the first priority of the new church is evangelism.

The Pastor's Responsibilities

Find new people

Once the new pastor begins to reach people, a second responsibility is placed on his desk. He must now try to keep as many of the new people as possible. Church growth writers refer to this keeping of new people as assimilation. Now the new pastor has two priorities to occupy his time, energy, and thought. He must continue to reach out and find new people, while trying to keep as many as possible of the ones he's already found. Thus the priorities on his desk now look like this:

The Pastor's Responsibilities

Find new people	Keep new people

At this point a third priority is placed on the pastor's desk. The pastor must now begin to coordinate a worship service and prepare and deliver a message.

The Pastor's Responsibilities

Find new people	Keep new people	Celebrate with people

What began as a simple task—finding new people—now has grown to include a fourth priority. The pastor must begin to train these new people. In most churches this new priority is referred to as Christian education. This priority includes the establishment of age-graded ministries, teacher training, and committees. The pastor's responsibilities begin to look like this:

The Pastor's Responsibilities

Find new people	Keep new people	Celebrate with people	Educate the people

As you can see, the number of responsibilities on the pastor's desk has increased significantly. Hopefully he has trained some of the people to take over a few of these responsibilities. But another responsibility is now added to these first four. By this point in the life cycle of a new church, several ministries have been started. These all cry out for oversight, and the pastor finds that he is being stretched by the demands of all the responsibilities he finds on his desk each morning.

The Pastor's Responsibilities

Find new people	Keep new people	Celebrate with people	Educate the people	Oversee the people

The pastor of our fictitious new church has much to keep him busy, but there's still one more responsibility that is placed on his desk. He now must care for the people that are part of the new church. When he first began planting this church, there were no people, so there were no hospital calls to make, no counseling to do, and no weddings or funerals to conduct. But now there are many needs, and the people push their concerns, calls, and visits on him in greater numbers each week. Now the pastor's desk looks like this:

The Pastor's Responsibilities

Find new people	Keep new people	Celebrate with people	Educate the people	Oversee the people	Care for people

It is certain that a new church plant doesn't develop in quite so linear a manner. Even so, this model is instructive as it provides an understanding of why churches begin to plateau and decline in later years as well as insight into how a church might be staffed to keep it growing.

Why does a new church grow in its early years but begin to plateau and decline in its later years? While there are several intersecting factors that we could point to, a major reason is the shift in priorities over the years. For example, in the early years of a new church, the priority is on the left side of the continuum, while in the later years the priority shifts to the right side.

Priority in Early Years   **Priority in Later Years**

Find new people	Keep new people	Celebrate with people	Educate the people	Oversee the people	Care for people

As the years go by, the church moves into a maintenance mode of taking care of what they have (people, programs, facilities) and abandoning the priorities that got them there (finding and keeping people and worshiping).

Insights for Staffing

This church-planting model gives us several insights into staffing a church for growth.

It teaches us that, as a church grows, the responsibilities on the solo pastor's desk become complex and numerous. A church with a solo pastor will stop growing when it reaches the limit of the pastor's ability to give adequate emphasis and time to all the priorities.

In the life cycle of most churches, the growing numbers of people already in the church will demand programs and care that will meet their personal needs. Pressure to provide for the people already in the church will force the distribution of money, time, energy, and leadership to the right side of the continuum causing the neglect of the left.

The tendency of most churches is to hire staff who serve functions on the right side of the continuum. Ultimately, staffing the right side of the continuum leads to an ingrown church that takes care of its own but neglects to find and keep new people.

A church that wants to grow will give priority to staff positions on the left side of the continuum. Staff who help find new people (evangelism), keep new people (assimilation), and lead in worship (celebration) will focus on the priorities that result in continued growth.

A senior pastor must understand his own strengths. If he is strong in areas on the right side of the continuum, he should seek to hire an associate who has strengths on the left side. If the senior pastor has strengths on the left, he should hire an associate who has strengths on the right, so the pastor is free to give his time to the priorities on the left.

All six priorities are necessary to provide a supportive environment for church growth. A church that seeks continued growth will not neglect any of these priorities.

A growing church will place a higher emphasis on the priorities on the left than those on the right. People in the church will adopt a servant attitude, which sees and responds to the needs of those outside the church over those already inside.

What is the best way to staff a church so that it grows? The answer is to staff a church from the left to the right side of the continuum. While there are numerous questions that remain to be discussed, it is hoped that this church-planting model for staffing will provide a new paradigm by which to view this important area of church growth.

41

ADDING PASTORAL STAFF

Research completed in the last half century has found that the order of a church's priorities often determines its growth or decline. Declining churches order their priorities this way: facilities, programs, and staff. Growing churches order priorities this way: staff, programs, facilities.

As a rule, a church may need to add staff if it answers yes to any of the following ten questions.

1. Is our church experiencing numerical growth?
2. Is our church on a plateau?
3. Are many things not getting done?
4. Do we have an assimilation problem?
5. Are there needs we should be meeting but are not?
6. Is our church becoming more complex?
7. Are there new ministry opportunities we would like to focus on but cannot?
8. Is there more to do than one pastor can handle?
9. Are we losing worshipers because our staff is too small?
10. Do we desire to move the church in new directions without ending current ministry activities?

Understanding Staff Ratios

The most helpful way to determine how many pastoral staff are needed is by comparing the ratio of staff to average worship attendance. Based on a half century of evaluation of churches with multiple staff teams, it now appears that a realistic ratio of staff to worship attendance is 1:150. Using this ratio as a guideline, the following table for adding staff may be helpful.

Professional Staff Positions

Average Attendance at Worship	Full-Time Staff Positions
150	1
270–300	2
390–450	3
510–600	4
630–750	5
750–900	6
870–1050	7
990–1200	8

What does this ratio of 1:150 mean? First, it means that each effective staff person tends to build a ministry that involves 125 to 150 people.

Second, it means a church desiring to grow to the next level should add a new staff person *before* reaching the projected growth level. This is a critical aspect of staffing that leaders often miss.

As the following table depicts, it is the addition of a new staff person that helps a church grow to the next level. For example, a congregation averaging 150 to 175 in worship attendance should be in the process of adding a second person to the pastoral staff, if the leaders expect their congregation to grow to 300 worshipers.

Professional Staff Positions

Full-Time Staff Position	Increases Church Size to . . .
1 pastor	150 people
1 + 1 pastor	300
2 + 1	450
3 + 1	600
4 + 1	750
5 + 1	900
6 + 1	1050
7 + 1	1200

Adding Support Staff

The number of support staff, such as secretaries, interns, or accountants, that a church needs depends on a number of factors. As a rule, more support staff are needed if the church is program-based, a large number of full-time professional staff are employed, or the pastoral staff are specialists. Fewer support staff are required if the church is cell-based, there is a large number of part-time staff, or the pastoral staff are generalists.

The following chart summarizes the need for staff in most churches.

Professional Staff Positions

Average Attendance	Full-Time Staff	Support Staff Positions
150	1	1
300	2	1.5
450	3	2
600	4	2.5
750	5	3
900	6	3.5
1050	7	4
1200	8	4.5

Other Considerations

Staffing ratios provide a good model for adding professional and support staff to a church. While ratios provide answers to some of the questions about adding staff, three additional overlapping questions are often asked: Should staff be added from inside or outside the church? Is it better to hire one full-time person or two part-time people? How much of the church budget should be designated for staff?

The Source of Staff

When answering the question, Should staff be added from inside or outside the church? a basic principle should be remembered: If change is wanted, hire from without; if change is not wanted, hire from within. If one of your purposes in adding a new staff member is to chart a new direction for ministry, the insider is least likely to do it. If, however, the ministry for which you are adding the new staff person is running well, and your main goal is to keep it running smoothly, the insider is a solid choice.

The Choice of Staff

Is it better to hire one full-time person or two part-time people? Part-time staff are an excellent choice if several conditions exist: The church has needs in several areas of ministry; the church is hesitant about adding full-time staff; financial resources are limited; the position calls for a specialist; the senior pastor is comfortable delegating work to staff; the position is temporary.

Full-time staff are the best choice in the following situations: It's obvious that the ministry needs someone who can work full-time, giving forty or more hours per week to the work; the position calls for a generalist; the staffing need is in one or no more than two areas of ministry; the senior pastor desires to spend time in one-on-one relationships and provide close supervision of the staff; the position is crucial to the long-term success of the church's ministry.

Budgeting for Staff

How much of the church budget should be designated for staff? Smaller churches tend to spend from 50 to 60 percent of their overall budget for staff, whereas larger churches typically spend between 40 and 50 percent. Taking into consideration that most churches are staffed for decline, it is a fair assumption that a church desiring to grow will spend more money and have a larger staff than represented in these averages.

42

Nine Principles for Hiring Staff

Pastoring a church that is experiencing significant growth has increased my learning curve in many areas. For instance, I've learned new skills for hiring staff. New skill development, however, comes with numerous mistakes. While there is great wisdom in learning from our own mistakes, there is greater wisdom in learning from the mistakes of others. So here are nine principles I've learned through trial and error for hiring additional staff:

Create a Shopping List

First, decide what the new position looks like and the knowledge a person would need to do the job. Examine the primary responsibilities of the vacated or new position and identify the ones that will require the most time.

Next, write a profile of the ideal person to fill this position so as to have a grid established for your evaluation. Ask the following questions: What specific education is needed? What vocational background is preferred? What depth of experience does this job mandate?

Then determine in advance not to lower your expectations no matter how desperate you feel. Evaluate all candidates against your shopping list, not against each other.

Use Team Interviews

Every résumé has its flaws. Many give a distorted picture of the real person. Rarely are a person's true strengths and weaknesses presented. Add to this the fact that a candidate is often able to fool a single interviewer, and you have the potential for a poor hire. However, seldom will a person get past a tag-team interview. Choose one or two other respected leaders, who share your vision and concur with the new job profile, to provide balance to the screening process. This not only increases morale and trust but also keeps you from being blindsided by surprises later on.

Ask Specific Questions

Explore several areas by asking targeted questions, such as, What are your strengths and weaknesses? What were the strengths and weaknesses of your previous supervisors? These two questions explore personal maturity in dealing with previous authority figures. Ask, What was your greatest success on your last job? What was your greatest failure? These two questions examine the candidate's ability to accept responsibility instead of placing blame. Questions, if appropriately designed, cut to the heart of the issues quickly.

Listen Carefully

After you ask a question, be quiet and let the candidate talk. I have found most candidates will tell you more than they want to tell you, if you are quiet. Intuition plays a major role in hiring new staff. If you have a "gut feeling" about someone, chances are you acquired this feeling while listening. Also listen for the person's use of pronouns. The use of "I" could be a sign of independence. When a candidate speaks in "we" terms, there is an implied familiarity with working on a team, and if this was the case in the past, the candidate will probably work well on a team again.

Take Notes

Those who are adept at interviewing have determined that we retain only about 75 percent of what we hear in an interview. If you interview several people, the chance of confusing your observations is great. Some companies have developed checklists to aid in the interview process. Other leaders have developed a shorthand code for their observations. Regardless of the technique you use, your notes will be crucial as you narrow down your search.

Look for Self-Starters

I have found there are many candidates whose qualifications fit a job description, but few who are motivated to go beyond expectations. Attempt to draw out of the candidate examples of projects he or she has completed and the results accomplished. Find out the process the person used to tackle the job, his or her work ethic while completing the task, and what he or she did when done. Proven producers will always produce. More than that, they have a work ethic that is contagious. In addition, most have the ability to motivate and empower others to follow their model for ministry.

Determine Passion

Many people can complete a task, but only those with passion can experience "kingdom" satisfaction and renewal. A candidate's *passion* is what he or she loves to do and what motivates his or her ministry. If you desire your new staff person to stay for the long haul, this person must serve in the area of his or her passion. Every organization has clock-watchers. Such persons rarely stretch beyond their comfort zone and usually are unhappy with their position and future. Seek to determine what empowers the candidate. This will quickly reveal his or her vision for work and passion for ministry.

Evaluate Followership

Sometimes a candidate has ability, education, and drive, but there is something you just can't put your finger on that scares you. You have picked up cues that indicate the person is not good at being a follower. This problem rarely surfaces during the courtship period on the job, but after the honeymoon is over and the person settles into the ministry, you may begin to notice a problem. Projects not completed are "somebody else's fault." Decisions that are disliked by the new hire are not addressed openly but behind the leader's back to other staff.

When hiring a new person, delve into this area of followership. Seek to determine how the person will react despite disagreement with a decision. A very penetrating question to ask is: What are some of the things you didn't like about your previous boss and why?

Establish Longevity

The number one reason many churches fail to fulfill their mission and advance the kingdom of God in their community is the issue of leadership tenure. Depending on whom you read, the average senior staff member stays at a church from thirty to forty-eight months. This has generated a leadership crisis in a majority of churches. If the position you are seeking to fill is vital to the ministry, longevity will be one of the keys to implementing this position successfully. Thus you must try to determine the future needs and aspirations of the candidate. Is there more education on the horizon? How long will it take for the candidate to become fully adept and functional in this position? Then what?

I know senior pastors who have never had to dismiss another staff member. For the most part, they are the leaders who have refined the hiring process. They know exactly what kind of staff person they are seeking and rarely experience the staff headaches we hear about.

Are there perfect hires? Not on earth! But using these principles will enable any leader to find the right person, with integrity and passion, who is ready to stretch and add skills to the team.

PART 15

SERVICE

43

A Culture of Service

One of my friends was pastoring a church that had grown dramatically during his first three years of ministry. He was an excellent strategist who effectively led his church to develop a plan for church growth, rallied church members behind it, and executed the plan flawlessly.

From most viewpoints it appeared the church would become one of the largest in his city within a few years. Technically all was in place for continued growth. However, by the fourth year, attendance had fallen significantly, and the church never reached the projections of growth that earlier had seemed so certain.

The reason my friend's church failed to reach its potential was that the people who were involved in it did not realize that *the heart of a growing church is service.*

The members' unwillingness to serve became obvious first in the evening child care ministry. As it turned out, no one was willing to watch the children on Sunday evening while other adults were involved in Bible classes. No matter what child care approach was attempted, people were just unwilling to serve in this crucial area of ministry.

Even though many mechanical aspects for growth were in place—plans, strategies, goals—the church suffered decline due to the people's unwillingness to serve one another.

Wanting the Best Seat

I share this brief story with you because I think it is important to stress that *the core of church growth is spiritual not technical*. All experience shows that even a superbly organized and planned ministry will eventually fail without the people's active care, love, and service for others.

People who need Christ will be drawn to our Lord because they see us loving each other (John 13:34–35) not because our techniques are sound. Yes, we need to be sure the strategic side of our ministry is solidly in place. People will be turned away from our Lord if we conduct ministry in a sloppy and thoughtless manner. But the underlying reason people are drawn to Christ is our loving service to each other.

Few would argue that churches are to be characterized by loving and sacrificial service. Christ made this evident when his disciples James and John and their mother approached him, asking to sit on his right and left side in his kingdom (Matt. 20:20–28). His answer set the tone of true ministry:

> You know that the rulers of the Gentiles lord it over them, and their great men exercise authority over them. It is not this way among you, but whoever wishes to become great among you shall be your servant, and whoever wishes to be first among you shall be your slave; just as the Son of Man did not come to be served, but to serve, and to give His life a ransom for many.
>
> Matthew 20:25–28

Creating a Culture of Service

A major part of a church leader's role is to build a church culture where people serve one another. Here are some general steps that others have used to build a culture of service in their church:

Commit to the long haul. Church cultures are notoriously slow to build and hard to change. Culture is an attitude that takes at least five to seven years to build up. It takes a lot of coaching, leadership, and example setting to see it become reality.

Acquaint all church leaders with your present church culture. Part of the reason it takes five to seven years to create a new church culture is that leaders must be educated to understand and see it.

Tap into the knowledge of your people. Spend a lot of time formally and informally asking questions, identifying values, and observing the way the church does things today. Write a description of your present church culture and identify what current values should be held onto and what new cultural values are needed.

Mold a new church culture. Read passages in the Bible that describe what a church should be and then verbalize a new cultural vision for your church based on what you learn. Before you can think about designing a new culture of service, you must decide what the new culture will look like.

Formalize your new culture. Begin by creating an official mission statement and a written set of values (see chapter 35). Calling people to a new culture of service will take place only when people understand and feel a sense of passion for the mission or purpose of their church.

Model the new culture. Leaders are crucial to a church's culture. Their words and deeds are its touchstones. Creating a positive culture of service means that leaders demonstrate concern for people already in the church, enhance their dignity, and help solve their problems quickly and fairly.

Communicate your new culture. Never force the elements of your new culture on people. Rather, concentrate on making steady inroads by communicating your new culture of service in a regular manner over a five- to seven-year period.

Reinforce your new culture. Use your church's newsletter to share stories of how members serve one another. Interview people from the pulpit who are living examples of the values of your new culture. Preach and teach on the value of service to each other.

Recognize people who embody your cultural values. Give an award, flowers, or a special pin to those who serve others. Publicly recognize people as quickly as possible so that others see that you believe in the cultural values you have verbalized.

Host an annual church event to highlight your culture of service. Take the opportunity to highlight your mission and values to everyone present. Give out several service awards and celebrate how God has blessed your church during the past year.

True Colors

Creating a new church culture is very much like painting the dark walls of a room with a lighter color. The original culture will keep bleeding back through unless people truly buy into the new culture.

You can write a new mission statement and develop a new slogan, but it's not the language; it's the attitude that's important. It's the depth behind the statements that counts. People's true colors will always bleed through any attempts to cover them up, and this is true of your church as well.

Capturing a new culture of service will be totally successful only when the hearts of your regular worshipers are committed to a new spirit of sacrificial service.

44

Putting People First

In the early growth years of the automobile industry, Henry Ford set the standard by using mass production techniques and standardized parts. He found that, by building only one type of car, he could produce it quickly and cheaply. His Model T was affordable, met most people's needs, and made Ford the major automobile manufacturer of the time.

Gradually people started asking for different models and colors of cars. Unfortunately, Henry Ford was not interested in putting people first. His response to requests for different colors was "People can buy any color car they want, as long as it's black." His failure to put people first caused Ford to fall from its number one position in car manufacturing as it lost market share. Perhaps this would not have happened if he had been willing to put people first.

If your church wants to grow, it must put people first, and when the leaders put people first, the people tend to grow in their commitment to serving each other. This phenomenon is called the "virtuous circle." When leaders put people first, the people tend to feel better about their church. In turn they put other people first in their own lives and keep the circle of loving care flowing from one to another.

A Most Important Question

The Peter F. Drucker Foundation suggests that a question all nonprofit organizations (including churches) need to ask is "Who is our customer?" Every organization has its own word for customer. Doctors call them patients, attorneys call them clients, and churches call them members and guests. But no matter which term we choose to use, serving people is what churches are called to do.

A church has two main customers—the person in the church and the person outside the church. Our "internal" customers represent those who already call our church home. Our "external" customers are the people we are trying to reach with the Good News of Jesus Christ. Since we have two types of customer, where do we place the priority in our efforts to put people first? It's not always easy to find the answer. It's a both/and situation. Putting people first means focusing on both of these customers. We must continue caring for those already in our church while at the same time reaching those outside our church.

Not Just a Program

Putting people first is not just a program; it's an attitude, a way of life. It means:

We must listen to people. By taking the time to talk with people, we demonstrate that they come first in the life of our church.

We take their concerns seriously. By going beyond simple acknowledgment of people's concerns to responding with action, we show people that their ideas are important.

We minister on their time schedules. By being sensitive to the lifestyles of our people, we communicate our understanding and concern about what they are facing in their everyday lives.

We are available in emergencies. By responding immediately in times of crisis, we tell people that they are our first priority.

We appreciate them. By thanking people, we express our need for them and their ministry.

We honor those who care for others. By praising people publicly, we hold up an example for others to model of how to put people first.

We accept them unconditionally. By lovingly accepting people as they are, we let them relax and share in Christ's forgiveness.

We challenge them to grow. By expecting people to mature, we support their desire to become all that Christ wants them to be.

Something to Think About

As we've seen, the secret of building a growing church is to put people first, which involves both an *attitude* and a *process.* Think through your church's commitment to putting people first by answering the following questions.

1. What is your church's attitude about putting people first? Use the items listed in the preceding section to determine this.
2. Can you identify specific actions or incidents that illustrate this attitude?
3. Are there ministries, programs, or other organizational processes in place in your church to ensure that people are put first in your ministry?
4. What are they?

5. Does your church give awards, honors, dinners, or other expressions of thanks to those who put people first in your church?

One way to communicate the value to your church of putting people first is to tell a true story. Here is an idea:

- Find one example from the past that shows the value of putting people first in your church's ministry.
- Write the example in the form of a brief story and read it to the entire congregation.
- If there are people still present in your church who were the ones illustrated in your story, present a framed copy of your story to them in front of the congregation after you read it.
- Use the story over and over again so that it becomes well known and a symbol of your church's legendary commitment to putting people first.

Think about the new ministries or programs you could develop to help reinforce this value. There are ways you can begin putting people first in your church even today.

45

THE NEEDS OF PEOPLE

An old Jewish story tells of a rabbi who asked the Lord to show him heaven and hell. "I will show you hell," said the Lord as he opened the door to a room. Inside was a large round table with a pot of delicious stew in the center. The people in the room were equipped with long-handled spoons, but they were starving. They were able to dip into the stew quite easily, but because the spoon handles were longer than a person's arm, they were unable to get the nourishing food to their mouth.

"Now I will show you heaven," said the Lord. This time the rabbi saw a room identical to the first, except that the people were well nourished, laughing, and talking. They had the same long-handled spoons, but somehow they had overcome their handicap. To the puzzled rabbi, the Lord explained, "It's simple but requires a certain skill—they have learned to feed each other" (From Glen Martin and Gary McIntosh, *Creating Community*, Nashville: Broadman and Holman, 1997, 25).

The people in heaven were obviously prospering in an atmosphere of giving and receiving. If someone had refused to give and receive, the system would have collapsed. This story clearly

illustrates a central need for members of any church—each
needs to be willing to give and receive.

Other Needs

There are other needs that a church must meet if it wants
the loyalty, interest, and best efforts of its members.

- *A sense of belonging.* The world we live in is marked by lone-
  liness. To combat the loss of community, some people go
  to nightclubs; others become overly involved in volunteer
  organizations; still others go anywhere they can to be
  around people—a daily visit to their bank or trip to a mall.
  God expects Christians to band together, caring, loving,
  and growing into a community where relationships are
  not superficial but penetrating and meaningful.
- *A feeling of purpose.* A feeling of purpose develops when
  members understand the biblical reasons for a church
  and their participation in it. Ministry and personal growth
  are most effectively accomplished through a company of
  Christians who are committed to Christ, to one another,
  and to ministry in the world.
- *An understanding of what is expected.* All churches have rules,
  often called norms, by which all members agree to abide
  while in the church. Members must have a part in determining these rules so they can live and work effectively
  toward the group goals. In some clear detail, church members must know what the church expects of them so they
  can confidently participate.
- *A part in planning the church's goals.* People need to have a
  part in the structuring of the church's overall plans and
  goals, a need that is satisfied when their ideas have a fair
  hearing. Goals and plans must be within reach. If members
  sense that the plans are beyond a reasonable ability to be
  reached, they will lose commitment to the church.

A challenging atmosphere. Time constraints on people of the twenty-first century dictate that they must make choices in the use of their limited time resources. To keep people involved in a church, they must feel that they are challenged in their thinking, that they are able to use their gifts within the range of their abilities and interests, and that their work in the church will lead to the accomplishment of its goals.

An understanding of what is going on. Members need to be kept informed. The things about which people are not informed are often the things they oppose. Keeping members informed is one way to give them status as individuals. Leaders usually think they are good at communication, but sometimes their listeners find they do not understand what is being said. A humorous story will serve as an illustration.

At the height of the vacation season one year, a trained investigator mingled with the crowds at Grand Central Station in New York City. He asked ten people, "What is your destination?" and received the following responses.

1. Protestant.
2. Mind your own business.
3. I'm a shoe salesman.
4. Home, if I can find my wife.
5. I'm learning to be a mail clerk.
6. Checkers.
7. Shut your mouth!
8. I don't know you.
9. Hoboken.
10. I believe in faith, hope, and charity.

Obviously, we must never just assume we have communicated to the members of our church. Get feedback. Make certain you're understood.

The Goose Story

In the fall when you see geese flying south for the winter, they will most likely be in a V formation. They fly that way on purpose. As each bird flaps its wings, it creates an uplift for the bird immediately behind. By using this flying formation, the entire flock adds about 71 percent greater flying range than if each bird flew on its own.

When a goose falls out of formation, it suddenly feels the drag of trying to go it alone and quickly returns to the formation to take advantage of the lifting power of the flock. As the lead goose gets tired, it rotates back in the formation and another goose flies the point.

If a goose becomes sick or wounded and falls out of formation, two other geese fall out and follow it down to provide assistance and protection. They stay with the fallen goose until it is restored to health and then together they launch out with another formation to catch up with the group.

If we have the sense of a goose, we will learn three things from this story about meeting the needs of those in our church.

- We need a common sense of direction, so we can get where we are going faster as we energize each other.
- We must stay together, taking turns doing difficult jobs and encouraging those who are leading the way.
- We need to stand by each other, helping to fulfill the six basic needs listed earlier so we all can move forward together.

PART 16

CHANGE

46

Bringing Change to a Church

Anyone who has watched people on water skis has observed skiers crisscrossing back and forth hopping over the wake created by the boat that is pulling them along. Jumping the small wakes created by ski boats appears to be easy. Water-skiers master the technique without much trouble and they always seem to have fun doing it.

One of the most popular innovations in water recreation has been the development of Jet Skis or SeaDoos. These small water vehicles allow the driver to sit, kneel, or stand up while he jets around a lake or ocean, much like water-skiers, but without the necessity of a towing boat. In lakes it is common to see these Jet Skis running over the wakes created by boats or other Jet Skis. But in the ocean, where the waves are much larger, it becomes more of a challenge. Still the people running the waves appear to have great fun.

Occasionally one of these wave runners will attempt a jump over an especially large wave or perhaps try to cross one at a wrong angle. When this happens, the craft often capsizes and throws the rider off. Fortunately the manufacturers of these water vehicles built in a device that causes them to stay in one place when the rider falls off, allowing him or her time to swim back to the Jet Ski.

Bringing about change in a traditional church can be as much fun as running waves in a lake. At other times, it can be disastrous. Sometimes changes cause fairly small wakes, like those usually traversed by water-skiers. At other times the wakes are much larger, like waves found in the ocean. Occasionally they become almost tidal waves, too powerful for anyone to jump.

As wave runners in our churches, we need to structure carefully a plan to effectively run the waves of change. Starting new ministries, restructuring older ones, or eliminating previously successful but dwindling programs is difficult in any situation but can be a major wave to jump in a traditional church.

The following ten steps are a composite of ideas and insights suggested by those who have run the waves of change before us in a traditional church.

1. *Bless the past.* Unless you are a church planter, you as a church leader are building on the foundation of others. It was their commitment, sacrifice, and love for the Lord that enabled your church to be where it is today. Always respect and honor the leaders who have served faithfully over the years.

2. *Affirm previous ministries.* Learn what ministries are legend in the history of your church and begin to affirm them and the people who served in them. This is particularly important to do with ministries that you are planning to restructure or replace.

3. *Stress principles not methods.* Highlight the foundational principles that undergirded past ministries. Think through each ministry that will need to be changed and identify the biblical principles that made it valid. Teach and preach those values and principles that are timeless and remain valid today.

4. *Present change as an extension of past ministries.* Present your new approach to ministry as an extension of a former ministry. For example, if you desire to begin a new worship service, focus on the fact that you are just expanding your present worship service so that it will reach more people.

5. *Illustrate how the change carries on values of a former ministry.* One church wanted to move from a midweek prayer meeting to a small-group ministry. The church leaders helped their people see that the value of the midweek meeting was prayer. As church leaders demonstrated that more people would be praying if there were several small groups meeting at different times during the week, the congregation agreed to give it a try.

6. *Assure people that you will be carrying on biblical principles.* Take time to educate people so that they understand it is the form of the ministry that is changing and not the foundation. Keep stressing the biblical principles of the past more than the styles of the past, transitioning into an explanation of how the newer forms carry on the old principles.

7. *Listen and love.* Leaders need to give people time to share their feelings, vent their frustrations, and become accustomed to the new ways of ministry. It is wise to provide small forums where a few people can ask questions, rather than have a full congregational meeting.

8. *Communicate that traditions are honored best when they are carried on in new ministries.* There are dead traditions and living traditions. The dead ones continue to be remembered but with little impact on life and people today. The living traditions continue on by providing the historical reason for ministries that are being accomplished in the present. The best traditions are the ones that point to the future through effective ministries that reach people today.

9. *Be patient.* Understand that in urban and suburban areas of the United States, it normally takes five to seven years to turn a traditional church in a new direction. In more

rural settings it often takes ten to twelve years and sometimes longer.

10. *Trust God to make it happen.* The old hymn says it well:
"O God, our help in ages past, our hope for years to come."
What better words to bear in mind while leading a traditional church? As we love God and his people, he will
help us bring about the necessary changes for effective
ministry.

47

Systems and Change

To comprehend events and processes in any ministry, we need to understand how people actually work together. One way to grasp how people, families, and close-knit groups function together is to see them as *systems*.

Thinking of relationships as a system may at times raise negative thoughts. How often have we heard the following?

The system works against us.

You can't fight the system.

People get lost in the system.

While systems can have a negative side, it is important for church leaders to accept and perceive that all organized human groups are in fact systems.

In this sense, a system is any group of human beings in regular contact with each other. Thus all organized human groups—families, service clubs, a circle of friends—have lives of their own and rules by which they operate.

We all live and interact with systems as a collection of related elements in a subtle and complicated way. For example, driving on a road, we are part of a system that interacts together through subtle expectations and rules of the road.

People who work, live, or minister with one another over a period of time develop patterns in their relationships, which are systems.

General Principles

Groups of people expect certain behavior from one another. The following general principles apply to most systems.

Systems behave as though they are persons with lives of their own. A human being is more than the cells that make up the body. In a similar way, when people join together as a group, they become a living system with a life greater than the individual lives of its members.

Systems act to preserve themselves. Any kind of change is perceived by a system as threatening and will be resisted, even when many individuals within the system are in favor of the change.

Systems maintain both external and internal boundaries. All systems have boundaries that divide the group from other systems. External ones control who gets in and internal boundaries control those within the system.

Systems are internally connected. Any action taken by a person in the group will have an effect throughout the entire system.

Systems maintain themselves by roles, rules, and rituals. The roles, rules, and rituals of the group work to bond members together and preserve the group for the future.

Understanding Change

While systems resist change, they can be transformed on two levels.

Level 1: First-order change. Changes that take place on this level tend to be minor ones and occur as the result of ordinary processes. These changes are the easiest to make and result in fairly minor disruption. For example, the color of the carpet is changed when the old carpet wears out, and new leaders are elected when older ones retire.

Level 2: Second-order change. Systems are capable of taking quantum leaps of change, but change at this level is difficult to accomplish and often requires a paradigm shift. Such changes occur in response to external and internal pressures. When a system is pushed far enough off balance, it will adapt itself to new ways of functioning.

A paradigm is a model, theory, perception, assumption, or frame of reference. It is the way we see the world. When the paradigm of a group changes because of external or internal pressures, it is called a paradigm shift. Here are some insights on making this kind of change:

- Paradigm shifts usually occur through a return to basic values and principles.
- Paradigm shifts usually occur over a period of time.
- Paradigm shifts usually occur from the inside out rather than the outside in.
- In a church, paradigm shifts usually occur as a result of Holy Spirit renewal, a change of leadership, serious disruption, and/or planned change.
- A first-order change usually involves surface attitudes, behaviors, and issues. If you want second-order change—a paradigm shift—focus on basic beliefs, values, and concepts.

General Strategies

Often a paradigm shift takes place through a planned process involving some of the ideas listed below.

Continuing education. Seminars and workshops are excellent ways to expose leaders to new concepts and move their thinking along quickly.

Hint: Always take a few leaders along with you when attending a training workshop or seminar.

Extensive reading. As a rule of thumb, it takes about 250 hours of reading about, thinking about, and discussing a new paradigm before it begins to be understood.

Hint: Accelerate the growth of your leaders by meeting once a week to discuss a chapter of a book that will help them understand the new paradigm.

Exposure to new models. Leaders often misunderstand a new approach to ministry until they see it themselves.

Hint: Ask your leaders to visit growing churches to see firsthand a new paradigm of ministry.

Diagnostic evaluations. Taking the time to analyze and evaluate the past, present, and future of your church is a sure way to open up a window of opportunity for change.

Hint: Involve your leaders in the process so they gain ownership of the results.

Five-year planning. By organizing a long-range planning team, a church forces itself to look to the future.

Hint: Build on the new century by establishing a vision team to plan for the future of your church.

Outside consultants. Using outside consultants increases the potential for second-order change to occur.

Hint: Schedule a series of consulting relationships over one to two years for maximum benefit.

Is your church's system open to change? Based on the above ideas, how can you begin to lead it in the twenty-first century?

48

Managing Change

Just because we develop a new vision for ministry, we won't necessarily see our vision realized. To see a vision become reality, we must actually do something. Changing a church's culture takes commitment, persistence, and time. A vision statement is just the beginning.

Keeping Vision Alive

People have to change and so does the infrastructure and systems that support them. Here's a simple look in principle form of what it takes to keep vision alive in your church.

Picturing the Result

The first principle: *What gets pictured gets done.* My wife loves to put together jigsaw puzzles. At holiday time we often retrieve a puzzle from our garage, we spread it out on a table, and the entire family works to put it together. One thing I've noticed is that it's easier to put the puzzle together when we first look at the picture on the box. Usually it takes us a long time to finish the puzzle, even when we look at the picture. I hate to think how long the pieces would be spread out on our dining room table if we didn't have a picture of the end result.

If you hope to empower a new vision in your church, you must paint a verbal picture of what you want for your people. Find a story that illustrates your vision and then tell it over and over until it becomes legend. Without reminders people will forget the vision within about four weeks, so talk about your vision for ministry every chance you get. Keep pointing people in the direction of God's vision for your church.

Modeling the Result

The second principle: *What gets modeled gets done.* To me the most frightening verse in the Bible is found in 1 Corinthians 11:1. In this verse the apostle Paul commands us: "Be imitators of me, just as I also am of Christ." People do imitate their leaders!

You can talk all you want about your new vision, but if people see you and other leaders behaving in ways that don't support your talk, you will find you are powerless. People are leader watchers, deciding what is really important by observing what leaders do. The excitement about a new ministry will gain momentum as people see you and other church leaders actually modeling your vision.

Reinforcing the Vision

The third principle: *What gets praised gets done.* People learn quickly what is applauded and what is not applauded in a church. If praise is given for cooking in the kitchen or driving students to camp, people will lean toward involvement in these areas of ministry.

Empowering a vision happens as you catch people fulfilling some part of the vision and reward them for doing it. Praise the behavior you want to reinforce, because the behavior that is reinforced is the behavior that is repeated; the behavior that is repeated becomes the prevailing attitude, which in turn becomes your church.

Training to Fulfill the Vision

The fourth principle: *What gets trained gets done.* The growth of a church is really the aggregate growth of its individuals. People do only what they know how to do. Usually adults want to learn the philosophy behind the vision as well as the skills to carry it out, so make certain your people know your mission, values, and philosophy. When you think about it, designing a new ministry is as much attitude as it is mechanics.

Train people in key skills that will aid in the fulfillment of your vision. If you are unable to do the training yourself, at least take responsibility for bringing in trainers from outside your church to do it for you. But be sure of this: A church that ultimately reaches its vision is one that nurtures people in a learning environment.

Measuring Your Progress

The fifth principle: *What gets measured gets done.* The only way we can ever really know if we reach our goals is to try to measure our progress. There's an old saying: "What is inspected gets done, not what is expected."

Empowering a vision requires the setting of standards and then measuring your results to see if you are matching up. Make sure your people know your goals and then measure your results each year to see if you're reaching them.

The key to long-term success is to continue setting your goals higher to keep your church moving forward. "Raise the bar," as high jumpers say. Constant improvement, even small improvements, is the only way to fulfill God's vision for your church.

Financing Your Vision

The sixth principle: *What gets budgeted gets done.* For any plan to come to life, enough money must be designated to make it happen. Each year, graph your budget by major categories and observe where the most money is designated. Then note where the least amount of money is spent. What priorities do your expenditures reflect? Are they what you want?

I estimate that most churches spend 15 percent of their money on things they don't need to do. To find more money, ask yourself three questions about every ministry in your church:

1. Why do we do this?
2. Do we need to do it at all?
3. Could we make better use of the resources we spend on this ministry?

What Are You Building?

A popular story that has circulated among leaders tells of a young traveler who came upon a laborer fiercely pounding away at a stone with hammer and chisel. The traveler asked the worker, "What are you doing?" The laborer answered, "I'm trying to shape this stone, and it's backbreaking work."

The traveler soon came upon another man chipping away at a similar stone, who looked neither happy nor angry. "What are you doing?" he asked. "I'm shaping a stone for a building," came the quick reply.

The traveler went on and before long came to a third worker chipping away at a stone. "What are you doing?" The worker smiled and replied, "I'm building a cathedral."

It takes a great deal of effort to develop a new vision in a church. When we focus on the backbreaking work, we may be tempted to give up, so keeping the proper perspective is a must. We are not just carving a stone, we are building a cathedral where God's love will shine as Jesus intended it to.

PART 17

GROWTH

49

PIONEERS VERSUS HOMESTEADERS

Anyone familiar with the history of the United States remembers learning about pioneers, who were the first to enter unsettled lands, and homesteaders, who came later to farm the land. As one can imagine, pioneers and homesteaders often found it difficult to get along with each other. The pioneers felt they had first rights to the land and resented the intrusion of homesteaders.

A similar scenario often takes place in churches when pioneers (old-timers) clash with homesteaders (newcomers). Sometimes referred to as a pioneer-homesteader crisis, this barrier to church growth can be found in churches of all sizes.

Lyle Schaller was the first to identify and use the terms *pioneer* and *homesteader* to define a church crisis. He notes that pioneers are usually the people who helped plant the church and thus share a number of firsts together, such as the first worship service, the first pastor, the first building, and so on. Pioneers are the people in a church who have a long tenure and close relationships, which allow them to control the church.

They are often called the old-timers and tend to be institutionally centered. The pastor is seen as their personal chaplain, hired to care for their needs.

In contrast, homesteaders are those who arrive after the significant firsts have taken place and thus have little or no remembrance of the "good old days." Since homesteaders have arrived rather recently, they don't have the long tenure or relationships that old-timers do. Often they feel left out of the church leadership, committees, memories, customs, and traditions. Usually they are ministry oriented, looking to the pastor as their leader.

Pioneer-Homesteader Crisis

A crisis develops when the pioneers in a church begin to feel they are losing control of "their" church. It occurs when enough homesteaders enter the church to threaten the power base of the pioneers. An "us-them" and "we-they" mentality develops between the newcomers and old-timers.

It is estimated that 80 percent of churches have experienced some form of pioneer-homesteader crisis. Ninety-five percent of pastors report experiencing such a crisis in their ministries.

An old-timer–newcomer fracture is a crisis for a church because it has the potential of being a barrier to growth. Generally a pioneer-homesteader crisis is likely to occur when one or more of the following are present in a church:

- The congregation has been in existence for more than ten years.
- There is a familial imbalance within the church where 15 percent or more of the people identify with one family.
- Eighty percent or more of the leaders on the main church board or committees are pioneers.
- The decision-making climate in the church is very emotional rather than rational.

If a pioneer-homesteader crisis is going to occur, it will usually happen within three years, but always within five years, of the initial influx of homesteaders into the church. In addition, the pioneer-homesteader crisis usually occurs when the number of homesteaders is equal to the number of pioneers or when the church increases 100 percent in size.

Surviving a Pioneer-Homesteader Crisis

The pioneer-homesteader crisis can normally be avoided if a church assimilates 50 percent new members every five years in an urban setting or every eight years in a rural setting. One experienced pastor suggests the following steps to work through such a crisis.

1. *Identify the problem.* The first task is to properly identify the problem. Is the tension in the church due to a pioneer-homesteader division or to some other source? Clearly identifying the issue provides rational handles to hold on to and presents proper solutions. As part of the first step, it is helpful to identify the opinion leaders of both pioneers and homesteaders, as these people are keys to resolving the problem.

2. *Adjust your attitude.* The pastor's personal demeanor is a highly visible model for the entire congregation during a pioneer-homesteader crisis. It is essential that a pastor demonstrate love, patience, and understanding during the struggle. One pastor suggests, "Be cool in the head, warm in the heart, and read Schaller."

3. *Prepare a plan.* Prepare an ongoing plan in four key areas: communication, education, motivation, and mobilization.

Proper communication should flow from pastor to people, people to pastor, and people to people. Lyle Schaller suggests that the pastor should seek to "depersonalize dissent," "seek agreement on short-term goals," "build a sense of mutual trust," and head off "escalating rhetoric."

Proper education should focus on teaching the congregation biblical principles for overcoming strife, assisting people to understand the particular dynamics of the church, and encouraging the pioneers to assimilate the homesteaders.

Proper motivation seeks to create a felt need for change, present positive goals, and exhort people to move toward those goals. In short, pioneers need to be motivated to open up and homesteaders need to be motivated to slow down.

Proper mobilization should help the congregation move beyond the pioneer-homesteader crisis. This usually involves a dividing and mixing of the pioneers and homesteaders in two worship services, new mixed Sunday school classes, or new mixed fellowship groups. Additional outreach ministries to bring more people into the church, as well as continual assimilation of newcomers, is necessary to avoid a future pioneer-homesteader crisis.

50

KEEP YOUR VISION ALIVE

On the morning of July 4, 1952, the California coast was shrouded in fog. Just a short distance to the west, on Catalina Island, thirty-four-year-old Florence Chadwick waded into the water to begin her attempt to become the first woman to swim the twenty-one mile strait.

Florence Chadwick was no newcomer to long-distance swimming. She had already become the first woman to swim the English Channel in both directions. On any other day she would have surely accomplished her goal. But on this day the water was numbing cold and the fog so thick that she could hardly see the boats in her own party.

Fatigue had never been a problem for Florence, but the extreme cold and the fact that she could not see beyond a few feet began to take a toll. After more than fifteen hours in the water, she asked to be taken out. Her mother and her trainer, who were in a nearby boat, encouraged her to keep going. However, a few minutes later, Florence asked again to be removed from the water.

Stepping on shore from her boat, Florence realized she had been less than one-half mile from reaching her goal. When a reporter interviewed her, she commented, "I'm not excusing myself, but if I could have seen the shore, I might have made it."

Florence had failed to reach her goal, not due to the cold or fatigue but because of the fog!

Three Ministry Fogs

Florence Chadwick's experience is common in all endeavors of life. Many church leaders can recount times when a fog caused a debilitating effect in their lives. As ministry leaders, we often experience failure due to three common fogs that cloud our vision:

- the fog of fatigue
- the fog of frustration
- the fog of fear

A good example of these three fogs is found in the Book of Nehemiah. When Nehemiah and the people worked to rebuild the walls of Jerusalem, Sanballat and Tobiah confronted them and attempted to discourage and ultimately destroy their work. As a result, the people experienced fatigue, frustration, and fear. How did they handle these fogs? How did they keep going to reach their goal? Nehemiah 4:9 gives us a clue: "But we *prayed to our God*, and because of them we *set up a guard* against them day and night" (emphasis added).

To see through the enemy fogs and accomplish their goal, Nehemiah and his people did two things:

1. They kept a spiritual focus (they prayed to God).
2. They managed the process (they set up a guard).

First, keep a spiritual focus. Maintaining a spiritual focus requires you to:

- *Take time to pray each day.* Jesus often slipped away to refocus his life in prayer (see Luke 5:16).
- *Keep the big picture in view.* Paul always saw the big picture and finished his race (see Phil. 3:7–16).
- *Focus on Jesus.* You must focus on Christ to keep from being distracted from your vision (see Heb. 12:1–3).

Second, manage the process. Managing the process requires you to:

- *Review your vision each day.* Remember, vision is an inside job. It starts inside of you! Write your vision down and read it three times a day—morning, noon, and night.
- *Share your vision with others.* Remember, when people buy into you, they buy into your vision! Meet with fifteen people a month and share your vision with them.
- *Recruit a team of visionaries.* Remember, achieving a vision is a team ministry. Find twelve to fifteen people who will join with you in making your vision a reality.
- *Get some rest.* Remember, rest gives us fresh eyes! Keep fresh by taking one day a month away from ministry for dream time and one weekend a quarter for physical, spiritual, and emotional rest.

The Rest of the Story

A few months after her first attempt to swim the strait, Florence Chadwick returned to Catalina Island to try again. The cold water and thick fog were still there, but this time she reached her goal. When asked how she was able to finish this second time, she reportedly replied, "This time the shore was in my heart."

Is your vision in your heart?

51

REACHING OUT

Hand out tracts, share "The Roman Road," invite friends to Sunday school, preach at a local mission, attend the Youth for Christ Saturday night rally, host a yearly revival, sponsor a vacation Bible school, and go door-to-door in the church neighborhood. All of these outreach methods have been effective in bringing people to personal faith in Jesus Christ. However, in the last half century there have been significant changes, which have made ineffective many of these highly regarded evangelism methods of the past.

Outreach Trends

In the middle 1800s the newest evangelism trend was the camp meeting. For at least three generations camp meetings were the most significant method for evangelism carried on in the southern frontier areas of the United States.

Today most church leaders wouldn't even consider using the camp meeting approach to evangelism. It is obvious that it was a method for an earlier time in North American history.

But what are the "camp meetings" of today? The following are five popular trends.

Target groups. Designing outreach events and programming for clearly defined groups of people produces better results than approaches aimed at broader audiences.

Church advertising. Advertising a church's ministry reaches people where they live and encourages them to attend church where they are exposed to the gospel.

Support groups. Offering various need-meeting support groups draws people into loving environments where they receive healing for their emotional hurts and hear the Good News of salvation in Christ Jesus.

Team evangelism. Teaming together with other Christians uses the special giftedness of each one in a cooperative effort to win people to Christ and eliminates the "me against the world" feeling often associated with evangelism.

Multimedia. Video, film, and tapes are ways to reach unchurched individuals in their normal patterns of life. People who may not come to a church event will listen to and watch Christian messages in their own home and car.

Increasing Outreach

While the basic need of people remains the same—to know Christ as their personal Savior—our changing world demands new approaches to win people to Christ. I suggest you implement some of the following ideas.

Build an evangelism consciousness. The heartbeat of an outreaching church must be Christ's goal—to seek and save the lost. A church without this basic consciousness will have difficulty reaching out to new people.

Implementation: Teach the basics of salvation and call attention to the needs of unchurched people in your community. For example, one church took all members on a tour of its community to expose them to the needs of unchurched people.

Pray for people's salvation. When church members hear their leaders pray for the salvation of unbelievers, it will increase their desire to begin praying for their own unchurched friends.

Implementation: Pray publicly for the salvation of people in general. Encourage all church members to pray for unchurched friends. For example, one church asked all its members to make a list of the unchurched people they knew and to pray for them daily for one year. Lists were turned in so that staff members could pray weekly for the same people.

Create name recognition. Often unchurched people don't have a high respect for churches. Growing churches create an environment in which unchurched people think positively about the church.

Implementation: Advertise your church's ministry to your target audience. For example, one church developed a first-impression piece and mailed it to every home within a three-mile radius.

Identify your primary target. Churches that reach people for Christ have identified their target audience and designed programs for that particular group of people.

Implementation: List the groups of unreached people in your ministry area, noting some specific felt needs. Then evaluate which group(s) God has gifted you to reach. For example, one church found its community consisted of 68 percent singles and designed several ministries to reach that specific target group.

Profile the unchurched in your area. Churches that are reaching new people for Christ understand the values and lifestyles of the unchurched people in their community.

Implementation: Develop a profile of the typical non-Christian in your community. For example, one church named the unchurched people in its area Community Cathy and Carl. They then listed five characteristics of Cathy and Carl and started new outreach ministries designed specifically for them.

Design presence evangelism events. An outreaching church will create a minimum of three ways to be present among its unchurched target groups.

Implementation: Begin one new ministry each year that will meet a specific need of unchurched people. For example, one church found that there was a need for an AIDS support group and started one for parents of AIDS victims.

Train church members. Generate a heart for outreach by offering continuous training in how to reach family and friends for Christ.

Implementation: Train 10 percent of your people each year to build friendships with unchurched people. For example, one church trains 100 percent of its new members and 10 percent of its long-term members to "Make a friend for Jesus."

A FINAL WORD

52

RESPONDING TO CRITICISM

Robert Kriegel and Louis Patler in their book *If It Ain't Broke—Break It!* say, "Pardon the grammar, but if it ain't broke today, it will be tomorrow. Today's innovations are tomorrow's antiques" (New York: Warner, 1991).

That's easy for a businessman to say, but how does a pastor in a local church handle the criticism that results from "breaking" old forms of ministry to use new ones?

Here are three pieces of information leaders need to understand:

Realize that criticism is inevitable. Students of physics tell us that any movement will produce friction. Since change requires movement, we can expect friction, which will bring criticism. It will come through the mail, in the hallways between services, via phone calls, and through third-party conversations. Just be ready for it.

Realize that some people will receive more criticism than others. Generally the more responsibility one has the greater the exposure to criticism. The Law of the Whale always

268

holds true: When you rise to the top and blow, you get harpooned!

Realize that pastors are magnets for criticism. There are many reasons why this is true:

- *Pastors confront sin.* Dealing with sin is a frontline activity, which naturally invites criticism.
- *Pastors create change.* Calling people to radical discipleship requires change in ethics, morals, and priorities.
- *Pastors give answers.* Giving advice is a common activity of pastoral leadership, but some people do not appreciate biblical suggestions.
- *Pastors are easy targets.* Critics seek safe targets who will not hurt them in return. Pastors usually do not retaliate.
- *Pastors appear strong.* Pastors put on a good front and, while they are often "in Christ" and "in church," they are in crisis. We are not as strong as we may appear.
- *People think they have a right to criticize the pastor.* Many people in local churches feel that they pay the pastor's salary and therefore can criticize everything he does.
- *People think they have a duty to criticize the pastor.* Some people feel they have an obligation to make certain that things at church are done right, according to their perspective.

Five Positives of Criticism

Some criticism is good, of course. Here are five positive or constructive results of criticism.

Criticism can create positive change. Often criticism causes leaders to focus on areas previously avoided or forgotten that genuinely affect the overall direction of the church.

Criticism can act as a unifying agent. The church at Smyrna (Rev. 2:8–11) is the one church of the seven churches listed without a condemnation. Why? These people banded together to face severe persecution and trials. Criticism can have a unifying effect on the body if properly addressed.

Criticism can force leaders to face unspiritual behaviors. Sometimes a church must deal with what I call "tare problems." The parable of the wheat and tares teaches that sometimes the tares look just like the wheat until they are full grown and then they must be dealt with. Criticism can point out problem behaviors among church attenders that leaders may not have wanted to face.

Criticism can clarify expectations. If listened to, criticism points to unspoken or unrecognized expectations. Once identified, these hidden expectations can be addressed and a better understanding reached between leader and followers.

Criticism can force the church to focus its vision. Criticism may reflect a lack of mission. One major reason conflict shows up in a church is a lack of vision. Instead of the people working toward a common good, they criticize anything and everything.

How to Handle Criticism

Dr. Grant Howard, wise trainer of pastors, suggests we do the following when facing criticism.

Apply the doctrine of admonition. Because I am imperfect, I make mistakes. Because I am in the body of Christ, I can expect to be evaluated by others in the body. No one grows apart from confrontation, correction, and criticism (Col. 1:28; 3:16).

Apply the doctrine of sovereignty. Failure is my problem. It is also God's program. When feeling like a failure, I must ask myself, *What positive things can I learn from this experience? What can I learn about people, Satan, my ministry, myself, the church?* Often truth is channeled through trauma (Rom. 8:28; 1 Cor. 10:13).

Apply the doctrine of relief. Eventually, relief will come. There is a way of escape, because his grace is sufficient. God wants me to have contentment and joy, not all of the time but enough of the time to allow me to enjoy life as well as endure it (1 Cor. 10:13; 2 Cor. 12:9; Philippians 4).

Apply the doctrine of forgetting. We can learn much from the past, without constantly living in it. After failure and criticism, we are even better equipped to move ahead (Phil. 3:13). Churchill said, "Success is not final, failure is not fatal; it is the courage to continue that counts."

The Bible says, "Therefore, my beloved brethren, be steadfast, immovable, always abounding in the work of the Lord, knowing that your toil is not in vain in the Lord" (1 Cor. 15:58). The "work of the Lord" involves both praise and criticism. As leaders, we must apply these doctrines as ways to understand and do the work of the Lord.

Pianist Arthur Rubinstein was fond of telling this story about himself. Never at a loss for words (he could speak eight languages), there was a time when Rubinstein was stricken with a stubborn case of hoarseness. The newspapers were full of reports about smoking and cancer, so he decided to see a throat specialist. After being examined, he searched the doctor's face for a clue, but the doctor told Rubinstein only to come back the next day. The pianist went home filled with fear. He couldn't sleep all night.

The next day there was another long examination and then an ominous silence. "Tell me, doctor!" Rubinstein cried out. "I can stand the truth. I've lived a rich, full life. What's wrong with me?"

The doctor looked him straight in the eye and said, "Mr. Rubinstein, you talk too much."

A wise physician once said, "I have been practicing medicine for thirty years, and I have prescribed many things. But in the long run, I have learned that for most of what ails the human creature, the best medicine is patient understanding of another's problems. And if that doesn't work, double the dose."

Dr. Gary L. McIntosh is a nationally known author, speaker, consultant, and professor of Christian Ministry and Leadership at Talbot School of Theology, Biola University, located in La Mirada, California. He has written extensively in the field of pastoral ministry, leadership, generational studies, and church growth.

Dr. McIntosh received his B.A. from Colorado Christian University in Biblical Studies, an M.Div. from Western C.B. Seminary in Pastoral Studies, and a D.Min. from Fuller Theological Seminary in Church Growth Studies.

As president of *The McIntosh Church Growth Network*, a church consulting firm he founded in 1989, Dr. McIntosh has served more than five hundred churches in fifty-three denominations throughout the United States and Canada. The 1995 and 1996 president of the American Society for Church Growth, he edits both the *Church Growth Network* newsletter and the *Journal of the American Society for Church Growth*.

Services Available

Dr. Gary L. McIntosh speaks to numerous churches, organizations, schools, and conventions each year. Services available include keynote presentations at major meetings, seminars, and workshops; training courses; and ongoing consultation.

For a live presentation of the material found in *Church That Works* or to request a catalog of materials or other information on Dr. McIntosh's availability and ministry, contact:

The McIntosh Church Growth Network
PO Box 892589
Temecula, CA 92589-2589
909-506-3086

www.mcintoshcgn.com
or
www.churchgrowthnetwork.com